UNIVERSAL WOMAN

Always with Love,
Diana

UNIVERSAL WOMAN

The Spiritual Feminist

Based on the work of
Reverend Ann Meyer, DD

A Collaboration of
Teaching of the Inner Christ, International
&
Diane L. Keyes

© 2017 Diane L. Keyes
All rights reserved.

ISBN: 1978487045
ISBN 13: 9781978487048

Original Dedication:
This book is dedicated to the Invisible One,
Who gave it to me line by line
At a time of my great need, And to all beautiful
Aware women, who are seeking more awareness of their true femininity.
A.M.

2017 Revision:
This book is dedicated to all women. Its intention is for the conscious co-creation of balance within the spiritual life that we may each fulfill our individual desires, unique purpose or calling, and become an example for Women of the 21st Century.
In Peace, with Grace

Table of Contents

Preface ix
Who is the Universal Woman? xi
What is a Spiritual Feminist? xiii

Lesson One	Universal Woman The Feminine Aspect of Life	1
Lesson Two	The Truth About the Universal Woman	11
Lesson Three	True Equality = Balance The Equality of a Woman in a Male-Female World	21
Lesson Four	Polarity and a Sense of Worth	33
Lesson Five	Universal Woman Desire and Your Physical Health	39
Lesson Six	Universal Woman The Creative Principle and Sexuality	49
Lesson Seven	The Partner You Desire	55
Lesson Eight	Acceptance of the Body Natural Poise – Grace - Lasting Youth	65
Lesson Nine	Love's Expression of Freedom	75
Lesson Ten	The Love Meditation	82
Lesson Eleven	The Universal Woman at Work Love or Fear?	88
Lesson Twelve	The Universal Woman in the World Spiritual Feminism	95

The Universal Gift 99
Teaching of the Inner Christ 111
Biography of Rev. Ann Meyer, DD 113
Bibliography & Recommended Reading 115
Acknowledgements 117

Preface

It was 1975, and my first connection with Rev. Ann Meyer, was by telephone. It was a call that changed my life forever. Her name and telephone number had been given to me by her son-in-law, composer, conductor and talent manager, Joseph Zito. At the time, we were in Toronto, Ontario, Canada. I found myself calling San Diego, California desperately seeking help for a sister, who had been diagnosed with cancer. Thirty days later, exactly as Rev. Ann had told me, the doctor apologized to my sister stating that they had made a mistake. There was no cancer. I was completely mystified.

Within months, we moved to California and I began a new spiritual quest. Over the ensuing decades, I stayed in contact with Rev. Ann, read and reread her books, took classes, and counseled with her regarding major life decisions.

In 1997, I gave a cherished copy of her "Woman Awareness" book to a publisher in Boston, Massachusetts. His response was that the book had great value, but it needed editing and updating. I called Rev. Ann with his review, and she said "...*and you are the right person to do the work.*" Wait – who? Me?

The publisher kept in contact occasionally to track our progress until, very suddenly, he made his transition. All hope for this project was diminished but never forgotten.

In 2007, while attending the Memorial Service for our beloved Rev. Ann Meyer, I once again received hope. One of the long line of people who came forward and shared their experiences with Rev. Ann, said that she had offered him a task for which he felt inadequate, unqualified and unworthy. She had told him, "*You don't have to feel worthy, you only have to be willing...*" I don't even recall the rest of his sentence. I heard her message loud and clear.

My prayer is that the new work on this book takes nothing away from its truth and that it reflects the progress we have made as women. Most of all...that I am simply its instrument, nothing more.

Diane L. Keyes

Who is the Universal Woman?

She is….
A woman who has mastered the balance between the masculine and feminine principles within.
She experiences the spirit of Beauty.
She understands Power with Equanimity.
She needs nothing as she has the Peace of God.
In that peace – there is no fear.
There is wisdom and grace.

She knows her worth.
She has her voice.

She knows God.
She knows the Presence of God in her body.
She knows the Presence of God in her mind.

She lives in the nature of a Christ.

She is….a Spiritual Feminist

What is a Spiritual Feminist?

She is a woman who takes her spiritual knowledge into the actions of her daily life.

She lays down the "fist" that has represented feminist social movements and replaces it with her heart and the Power of Love.

She understands that she is a whole woman, functioning in the world with both masculine and feminine aspects as given by the Creator of all Life.

She knows that in healing herself, she heals others.

She knows how to make a difference in the lives of others through her Divine Wisdom.

She is fearless, knowing and expressing the innate God-given Power that lies within.

She thinks globally, understands our connectedness, and prays with all women for honor and respect.

Her campaigns are based in the power of Love and create pathways to peace…

…therefore she cannot be denied.

This book is about you …individually and in unity with all women. It is time to see all women – worldwide – as the feminine nature of all humankind. It is time to be inclusive in a world vision, where the powerful feminine nature of all Life creates peace in Oneness with each other.

Times have changed and social customs, traditional gender roles, and relations have evolved. Striving for social justice is continually moving to the forefront of our consciousness.

This book invites you to know yourself and your power as a spiritual force. We can achieve social justice with splendor and harmony. It need not be another war.

The seven major religions of the world have much in common. For thousands of years, each of them have taught ethical behaviors regarding honesty, loyalty, larceny and violence. Humanity as a whole has fallen short in achieving these basic conducts. We can do better.

You are the answer - With the vision of a Universal Woman, you can lift yourself and together we can lift each other.

In our pursuit of expanded self-awareness, let us begin – at the beginning… with God. This course is based on metaphysical principles, and we begin with the concept that God as Universal Spirit, is All Power, All Intelligence, All Love, and is Omnipresent – in all, through all, as all. There is no place where God is not. It is **impossible** for you to be separate from God. All is Oneness, and that Oneness is God, the Creator, our Higher Power, our Father-Mother God, Universal Spirit that creates through the instrument of Universal Mind. Use whatever terminology with which you are most comfortable. It only matters that you realize the nature of your relationship to this magnificent Power and Presence that we call God.

There is the concept that God is Love and in the power of that Love, all things are possible. What you cannot do – God can. These are the words of faith that buoy us to constantly flow forward. Being a woman of deep faith can create miracles. If you do not have that level of faith now, then lean on ours. We are available to you.

Read the following lessons and be diligent in the practices. We suggest one lesson or chapter, per week. If you stop somewhere along the line – start again from the beginning. Ten weeks is a short time to transform your life. If you get stuck - call us, or contact us through our website. (See Page 104) You will experience change where you most desire it and build faith in yourself in the process.

You can and will stop thinking there is something wrong with you. You will realize that your life matters to God, and you matter to us. We women belong to each other. Your transformation is at hand. Lay down your struggle, accept the truth and be exceptional.

> *"Beauty is a feeling. It is a rapport, a tuning, translated into sight or sound. Beauty is a oneness, a recognition of your soul, a speaking to yourself in another person, place or experience, a recognition of God and of life. "*

JESUS' LOVE
BROTHERHOOD OF THE FOLLOWERS OF THE PRESENT JESUS

Before you begin...
Rev. Ann Meyer's original book, <u>Ten Lessons in Woman Awareness</u> was published in 1968 as a spiritual guide to Feminism and was a loving response to the rebellious and often angry nature of the women's movement. It told the truth about their feminine nature, true beauty and sexual freedom. Rev. Ann gave women an opportunity to redefine themselves from a new spiritual perspective. This new ten week course promises that and much more. It shows what may be accomplished when we make sacred choices from the heart.

   Rev. Ann also wanted to make it clear that the oppression of women did not come from God. Each of her original lessons provided biblical references to impress this upon the student. We are empowered by God, not dominated or manipulated. This new edition will add references supporting the same, including quotes and references from multiple religions as well.

As successful as organized women's movements have been, women are still "fighting" for equality and respect. Fighting can be exhausting. We want this book to teach you to master the art of "co-creation". We can do this together and co-create significant advances for women.

Huston Smith, renowned author and professor of world religions, writes in *"The Meaning in Human Existence"* - *"The most crucial element in a people's outlook is in their self-image. Human nature from maggot and worm to crowned with glory and honor – born a guilty sinner- or child of God – A God of Love"*.

The culture of our society in the U.S. has changed greatly since the first edition of this book. Women have made their mark in areas our mothers would not have even dreamed of fifty years ago. Women are in powerful leadership positions worldwide for the first time in our modern history. Yet women have paid a dear price for these freedoms. Violence against women is still rampant worldwide. Our culture today has become a "love/hate – good/bad" mindset. We are still not as united as we can and must become in order to reach our potential as women. We can and must do this together.

For the last few decades in the U.S., women have been seeking the answers to how to balance career and family responsibilities. Fulfillment in one area sometimes has left much to be desired in another. Whole industries have been built around what's been missing for the hard working woman. Now, as successful career women, we must fit into a certain size pants, be well manicured and carry a designer handbag. In the U.S., we have become a culture that values wealth, power and physical beauty, sometimes in mysterious ways.

Women will find their potential from an entirely new perspective when we learn to balance our mental – physical – emotional – and SPIRITUAL – needs. All of this can be accomplished as we understand our true woman nature.

In our growing awareness of the oppression, suppression, and nothing less than the horrors of violence toward women around the world, we ask how this could continue for centuries and what could we possibly do to create a change.

The answers are the same today as it was for Rev. Ann in the 1960's and as it always has been…Education and the **realization of our true nature**, so that we may grow in consciousness.

When women live in fear, we make poor choices. We must learn of our true power.

When women know the Source of their strength, we will cease to be intimidated.

When women learn to love and respect themselves, all our relationships will improve.

When women learn true compassion, we will teach it to our sons and daughters.

So here we are fifty years after the first publication of Rev. Ann Meyer's work on behalf of women, applauding the tremendous strides made by women all over the world, with the hope that this material will further the journey to the fulfillment of equality, true to our full feminine nature, powered by Love.

We must also acknowledge the marked fundamental progress made by men as a result of the women's movements. Most men of this current generation have become more enlightened partners, with greater participation as husbands and fathers than the generations before them. This is more natural than you think. Thank you, God!

At the close of each of these lessons, you will find a series of affirmations to work with that will help you adjust your belief systems about yourself and others. Your words are powerful. The words we speak affirm our thoughts and create beliefs. Recently, I had the occasion to visit three of the largest national chain stores that are purveyors of arts and crafts supplies. I found myself amazed at the number of displays of ready to hang, positive affirmations in all shapes, colors and sizes. Your entire home could be filled with spiritual support. This is a testament to a nationwide acceptance and belief in the power of affirmative words. Thank you, God…and to think – it only took two thousand years.

Many organizations consider themselves part of the "New Thought" movement. Yet that term was coined over a hundred and fifty years ago. When is "new" considered "old"? Obviously, not by calendar, but by relevance. To those who took this course from the first edition, you will find omissions and enhancements. Even as the lives of women have changed significantly in the past fifty years, some things still remain to be clarified.

If you do not yet have a daily spiritual practice, we urge you to use this book to begin one. What better way to begin redefining yourself than to start your day in communion with your Creator. One possibility is to try rising in the morning an hour earlier before anyone else in your household. Find a place where you may light a candle, say a prayer, meditate, and say your affirmations. Journaling in this part of your day is another aspect that not only can track your progress but become your personal letter of gratitude for your new realizations and also set your intentions for the day. If an hour seems undoable, start with an amount of time you feel is best and work your way up from there. The point is to start.

You may want to print some of the affirmations from the lessons and place them around your home and see how they influence even those with whom you share your life. When you incorporate them into your daily spiritual practice, try to *feel* what these words mean to you. That feeling is an essential key to your progress. *Visualize* yourself as the whole and complete woman that lies within. It doesn't matter what your "earth age" is – your divinity is eternal.

This material may be explored as a group, or as in an individual spiritual journey. There are many who are available to lead you through this material. You will find their contact information at the end of the book. Each of us want you to move from wishing and hoping to knowing and being.

Many churches have trained Prayer Partners, Prayer Therapists, Prayer Chaplains, Practitioners, or Prayer Teams to assist you. For the purpose of this book, we will use the words Prayer Partner to include all those pray with you on your spiritual path.

As we grow in consciousness, so does the world…

In Love….

LESSON ONE

Universal Woman
The Feminine Aspect of Life

"To Love beauty is to see Light"

– Victor Hugo, French Poet, Novelist, Dramatist

World leaders proclaim great needs for humanity such as peace, freedom from poverty, better education, better government and other issues, but few have realized the greatest need; a deeper understanding and acceptance of the true Feminine Nature. If the true feminine or feeling nature of all humanity were freed to express in balance with the true masculine nature, then war, cruelty and greed would, as a natural consequence pass out of human thinking.

Women today, are finding greater freedom and power, yet they also feel a great need for balance. Through a deeper exploration of the Universal Woman nature, we are able to express more of our innate femininity, to enjoy ourselves and men more, and to break free from the heavy mental, emotional and physical restrictions which have bound us through the ages. These bonds can be broken only through more meaningful understanding. This understanding must begin in the minds of women themselves.

This series of lessons is designed to open your awareness of the Universal Woman within you. For there is a beautiful, wonderful, glorious woman within, waiting to express though unlimited love. You can peel off the layers of misunderstanding and rejections that bury her and the true woman within each of us.

As you begin this course in understanding the Universal Woman, it would be wise to determine just what you wish to gain from it. We live in a universe of spiritual power directed by a Divine Mind. It is well to clearly define what you desire. This will make a corresponding demand on Universal Power. If you follow through with your study each day, never wavering until you achieve the fulfillment of your goal, or specific desire. We dare to promise this, because it is a Universal Law. Be prepared for one thing, for in the process of achieving your goal, your life may change. The change will be for the better. How could an increase of self-awareness bring anything except a higher good?

The following is a list of possible goals, which you may work toward during this course. Record your choices in a journal. You may add to the list as you progress, for you alone know your individual needs.

What This Course May Bring to You:

> Greater self-acceptance; and self-confidence
> Greater joy in living
> Clarity of purpose
> Peace of mind
> Greater ability to express yourself; attracting more love
> A greater experience of beauty – both inner and outer beauty
> Finding your own voice
> Greater balance in your career
> Understanding your own power
> Harmony in relationships with both men and women
> A more balanced relationship with your partner
> Better self-care; improvement in your personal environment, etc.
> Fuller expression of sexual love
> More flexibility and spontaneity in your life
> Freedom from mental, emotional and physical bondage

Underlying all problems is the one problem of self-acceptance. Everyone around us accepts us – Life accepts us – to the measure that we accept ourselves. We set the patterns for our life experiences by what we believe ourselves to be, by what we believe we are worthy of receiving, and what we believe we can become. If we are to have fuller, happier lives, we must first increase our self-acceptance. We can do this through more awareness of who and what we really are. Each of us is so much more than any of us realizes.

Universal Divine Mind has different functions. For instance, consider your own hand. You can push or you can pull with it, but it is still the same hand. This Divine Mind can function in different ways and still be one Mind. Indeed, Universal Mind enters into the creative process by separating itself into two opposing functions which work with one another to produce a created result. The Creation story of the Earth itself gives us this principle. As "In the beginning was the Word" (One function of God-Mind) which was placed into Spirit "moving upon the waters" and the Earth came into form.

Everything in the physical world, began with an idea. Somewhere in the mind of the Inventor, in the intelligence within an apple seed, or within the minds of a man or woman and a soul waiting to incarnate, these ideas were given expression through a medium, a way of manifestation, and became a created form. You have access to the Divine Mind where inspiration is infinite. Divine Ideas (Cause) through Medium (or Mind Activity), creates Effect. Ideas placed into Universal Power is an act of creation.

Affirmative Prayer, is based upon the principle that Word spoken into Spiritual Law creates its manifestation in the world. A physical application of this creative principle is the interaction of a man and woman creating a physical body for a new child. The male projects into the female, just as the Word projects into Spiritual Law. The Feminine Nature and Spiritual Law both have as their function, the act of acceptance, and nurturance to the implanted seed, thus giving birth or manifestation of the original idea.

Every object, experience, or manifestation is created in this same way. The masculine aspect of mind, works upon and through the feminine aspect for all creation. All actions in life, be it spirit, mind or body is masculine and feminine action. Sex is the principle of life's creative action in every field of expression. Sex is not what many have judged it to be –a means of physical gratification. It is sacred.

Nature shows us this principle even in the trees. I once had an avocado tree that was not producing its fruit. Concerned that the tree was in trouble, I contacted a nursery to inquire about what action I should take to correct this situation. I was told that the corresponding male tree (in someone else's yard) was most likely cut down and my female tree lost its partner. This was a literal "birds and the bees" moment in Dendrology… God's Universal law.

It is a Universal principle, a spiritual Idea. It is God in creative action at all times, and everywhere. The physical symbol of the spiritual creative action for humans is in physical acts of lovemaking. As we realize this as a representation, we can begin to see it as a marvelous, glorious expression of God.

As women, we are the expressions of the Feminine Aspect of God. We represent the **Medium** of creation, the Holy Spirit, the Soul, the Power, the Love aspect of God. Each human being, whether male or female, is an individualization of a Universal God, having all of the aspects and qualities of God…just as a drop of ocean water has all of the properties, of the ocean. Each person has all the qualities of the whole, in the entire illustration, the Wholeness of God.

As Universal Women, we are made in the image of the Feminine Aspect of God. We are the Feeling Nature of Love. We are the beauty, the tenderness, the receptivity, of Universal Mind. As God is LOVE - We are LOVE. .

Anecdote from Rev. Ann: Each of us women chose to be a woman before we were born into this lifetime. Whenever this statement was made in a Woman Awareness class, at least one woman cried out, "Do you really mean that I chose to be a woman?" At this point, many women have confessed that they always secretly wished they had been born a man. Then, a few lessons later, they invariably claim, "For the first time in my life. I'm <u>glad</u> I am a Woman!"

We believe that God *is* Love, and the power of Love in ways beyond our comprehension. It stands to reason that this is a universe of individual choice, as Love surely includes respect for all expressions of life, and surely Universal Love does not work through force or dictatorship. On some level of being, we chose to come into this lifetime to express as a woman.

Deep within each of us is a whole and complete Spirit Being, a perfect individualization of God. Our outer personality is wrapped around this Self, like a cloak, or series of cloaks, which to a great extent hide the Inner Self and make us appear to be quite different from what we really are inside. The outer person may appear to be unattractive, misshapen, fearful, or ill, but the Inner Self is always whole and perfect.

A fact, is a statement about the outer self. An affirmation, is a statement about the Inner Self. If we make affirmations of the perfection of the Inner Self – often and with belief – the outer self will comply and become more like the Inner Self. Thus by using the Universal Woman Affirmations in this book daily, we begin to change our outer persona and our bodies to conform to our inner Truth. This is not difficult to achieve. Merely say the affirmations with all the feeling you can muster and you will create belief that will prove that life can change. Unity Worldwide Ministries teaches that - *Thoughts held in mind produce after their kind.*

Many of us may have lost touch with the idea of inner wholeness to the extent that the affirmations of Truth will, at first, seem like absolute lies. Say them anyway, even if you can't believe them. As you say them daily, your belief in them will grow in your subconscious mind and will become creative. This is not about vanity, conceit, narcissism, or the ego. What you are claiming for yourself, is the realization of your inner self, your highest self. Only you - can teach your subconscious mind.

It is wise to find a special time of the day for your Universal Woman study and mental work. A good plan is to concentrate on one lesson per week. Carefully study the affirmations at the end of each lesson. Each lesson is designed to build a consciousness of self-acceptance and prepares you for the next lesson. To achieve the greatest results, study each lesson in the order they were written.

All Affirmations are printed in order, in the last section of this book, beginning on page 90, titled "The Universal Woman Treatments".

As you progress from chapter to chapter, lesson to lesson, you will begin to notice positive changes in your attitudes and relationships. Ten weeks from now you may have an entirely new perspective on yourself as a truly remarkable woman.

Begin your work by saying the first week's affirmations as listed and defined below. Once you understand their meaning, you may proceed to the "Lesson One" list in the last section of the book. Say them with conviction, and enjoy your first week.

The Universal Woman
Explanations of Affirmations

I am Life – God, expressing as a Woman.
God - expressing as a woman does not mean that I am superior or more powerful than others. Science tells us that a drop of the ocean contains all the ingredients of the entire ocean. Like that drop of water, I have within me, ingredients of God. I am not all of God, but am an expression of God, in the form of a person – a complete man-woman person, and in this life, have taken the form of a woman.

Another way to see this is through the works of a great artist. Think of the works of the French Impressionist Claude Monet. His works of art are some of the most famous and recognizable in the world. Each of them is an expression of him, and when you see one of his works, you see it as "a Monet" regardless of its subject matter, colors, or size.

Scientists state that each person has the physical characteristics of both sexes, with one sex dominating and the other dormant. Our inner nature, also has both male and female characteristics. As a woman, the woman nature is dominate. This does not mean that we do not use our masculine natures. As 21st century women we express both natures more than any time in history. As a result of greater functioning in a male dominated culture, we now strive for balance.

I am the Feminine aspect of God, I am a Universal Woman
Since, I am an expression of God, having qualities of God within my Being, expressing the feminine nature of God, I have all the qualities of the Universal Woman. I was created in the image of the feminine aspect of God. I have every womanly quality possessed by any woman in the world. As you say this affirmation, try to feel, in every cell of your body, Universal Femininity.

I am complete and whole Woman.
I have everything within me, which God's idea of Woman, includes. I lack nothing. I release any former thoughts or beliefs of inadequacy. Even if any physical part of the body has been removed, the inner bodies are forever intact and I am whole, perfect and complete.

I am pure Woman, authentic and true Woman.
The word pure, in the affirmation is not meaning "morally chaste". It means I am all Woman. As an authentic and true Woman, I am true to myself. As we become more aware of the true Woman within us, and gain the feeling of this true Woman, we will express our true nature freely and naturally in ways that may even surprise us.

I am a free, natural Woman.
I am free to express my natural woman's desires and feelings. This does not mean I may trespass on another, or that I am free <u>from</u> someone or some experience. It means that I free myself to express more woman love than ever before. Freedom in my life experiences will come as the natural result of my new mental freedom, for all freedom begins with the inner self.

As you continue with this affirmation, you will discover the expression of the "natural woman". The Angels, or Higher Beings, who live in higher realms of vibration, are incredibly, wonderfully, unashamedly natural. Their walk is free, and natural. They exhibit pleasure in themselves, their bodies and are gloriously and joyfully sensual.

I am the Essence of Femininity.
This powerful affirmation may create change in just a few days. You may reassess your personal style; make changes in dress or your hair; or reevaluate your environment – all from a genuine desire to reflect the beauty within you. Think of yourself as the Queen of the Universe! Something pleasant will surely happen.

Choose a quiet spot, sit and relax, and say these affirmations with meaning, belief and feeling. Say them aloud. Try to do this at the same time each day. Take your time, and be diligent. You are reeducating your subconscious mind, know that this will change your life for the better. This is truly worth your time and effort, and will create some of the most enjoyable moments of the day. You will be richly rewarded with new and greater happiness.

Please refer to the illustration "The Masculine and Feminine Aspects of Being" in the back of the book (Page 110). It presents the idea of two basic yet differing aspects of Universal Mind which work together in the creative process. Cause through Medium (Mind Activity) creates Effect. An idea, placed into Universal Power manifests after itself.

Universal Woman Treatment 1

I am Life – God expressing as a Woman.

I am a complete Male-Female Being, expressing as a Woman.

I am the feminine aspect of God. I am Universal Woman.

I am complete and whole Woman.

I am pure Woman, perfect Woman, and true Woman.

I am free, natural Woman.

I am a unique, individual expression of all Woman.

I am the essence of femininity

Notes

LESSON TWO

The Truth About the Universal Woman

"A billion stars go spinning through the night,
blazing high above your head,
but in you is the Presence that will be, when all the stars are dead"

RANIER MARIA RILKE, POET 1875- 1926

GREETINGS, UNIVERSAL WOMAN! If you have done your spiritual work with the affirmations from Lesson One, we know that changes have already been made within you. Even a small change indicates that you have a new awareness of your woman nature and this is progress. By now, you will begin to have a clearer feeling and knowledge of the masculine and feminine principles of the universe.

It is important to clear our minds of any prejudices, false judgments, or prevailing thoughts about women which simply have no basis in truth. They only serve to limit or block our fullest expression of life and love.

Religions have contributed greatly to general misunderstandings about gender roles and the principle of sex. Various teachings have supported the theory for people to limit or reject their sexuality and thus, both men and women have rejected themselves.

As we examine this opening story of the English version of Hebrew Scriptures, we see immediately that we have ascribed a gender to God. Names for God—*Yahweh, Elohim, Shaddai, Sebbaoth, Adonai, Kurios,* and *Theos*—are all masculine gender. The prophet Isaiah of the Old Testament, and Jesus in the New Testament, have also attributed feminine references to God. Books sourced by several ancient religions, praise the Divine Feminine.

Whatever your description or understanding of God is, know that we as human beings have limitations as to our ability to comprehend the Creator. There is no pronoun for God. Please keep that in mind as you read the following story.

Ask yourself – Does God have gender or have we in our limited thinking, assigned the male pronouns to God? The French born author Genevieve Behrend (student of New Thought co-founder, Thomas Troward) defines God as a Supreme Power, back of, underlying, and in all things. It is Infinite, Eternal and Unchangeable. It is Omnipresent, Omnipotent, and Omniscient. This Supreme Power may also be called Mind, Spirit, Law, the Absolute, First Cause, Nature, Universal Principle or whatever name best suits your desire to explain or understand God. In our desires for a more personal relationship with the Creator, the word "It" hardly seems acceptable, so "He" is what scriptures used. (Of course, the majority of the authors of religious scriptures were men.)

As Christianity termed God as a loving father, it allowed one to pray with love and affection, as opposed to fear and supplication. One might also feel more deserving in a relationship to a Father-God. Another trait of the "Father-God" is that this concept affirms that as His children, we are all of one family. We are not separate from each other but literally sisters and brothers. Many New Thought churches use the term Father-Mother God to view the attributes of the Creator as whole and balanced.

Award winning British author and Catholic feminist, Sara Maitland, writes in "A Big-Enough God", "God created diversity in humanity and diversity in sexuality. We must understand that these differences are desirable."

Perhaps instead of subscribing to one particular description of God, one should simply focus on the *experience* of God. How much more then can we learn about Love and Life?

It is also beneficial to embrace our uniqueness as much as possible, without becoming so individualistic that we lose our connectedness to each other.

Let us look at gender using Rev. Ann Meyer's example from Biblical scripture in Genesis, Chapter One, the story of creation and the Garden of Eden.

This story furnishes the best pattern to show us the effects of judgement in our lives. It does not matter whether you believe this story as history or allegory. It is a lesson in states of consciousness and its effects. This story presents the process of creation and how it can be distorted by the judgement of good and evil. The Adam, Eve, and the "apple" pattern constantly repeats itself within individual minds, while Spirit seeks to restrict judgement.

The book of Genesis, Chapter One reveals the glorious process of all creation. Spirit (God-Mind) dividing Itself into masculine and feminine aspects ("Let us make man"), the speaking of the Word into the Law, ("Let there be light") followed by the demonstration ("And it was so") and the pure acceptance of the result (And God saw that it was good"). Notice verse 27; "So God created man in His own image, in the image of God, He created him; male and female, He created them."

Some scholars interpret this chapter believing that at first, the human was both sexes in one. Later, they are male and female. Notice also, that God, after creating them, did not command them to "be good" or to "behave themselves", nor did God give them any rules of conduct. They were told to "Be fruitful and multiply, and fill the earth, and subdue it and have dominion over the fish in the sea, and over the birds of the air, and over every living thing that moves upon the earth." We may take these creatures of the sea and land to represent the thought of human consciousness, over which we are to take command, and to subdue our environment, (the earth) and gain dominion over the experiences of our lives. All of these thoughts are to be fed, God says, by "every green plant for food" (Universal Energy).

Chapter Two presents either a second story of the creation of man, or else an account of the creation of the outer man, in contrast to the story in Chapter One, of the creation of the inner man. Biblical scholars differ on this. Read through verse nine, the story of the Garden of Eden, which represents the mind of the newly created man. In this fresh pure male-mind, there was every tree that was pleasant to the sight and good for food. (Pure thoughts), also the Tree of Life (Universal Mind Power) in the midst of the Garden, and the Tree of the Knowledge of Good and Evil (the tree of judgement, duality of thinking). Fear was born here.

It is a good thing to have discernment in the mind. It is how we distinguish distances or make accurate measurements. There would be no science, organized knowledge or skills. Discernment is choice or evaluation, without pronouncement of good or evil. The Tree of Judgement is a necessary part of our "Garden of Eden" (our minds). It is only when we _feed_ upon this tree, using this faculty to brand ourselves as good or bad, successful or failing, that our minds become confused and fearful.

Let us read verses 15-18. Man was instructed to till and to keep this garden (of his mind) and to freely eat of all of the trees (freely feed upon inspirational thoughts) – All except the "Tree of Judgment". "For in the day that you eat of it, you shall surely die." Now man _did_ eat of it, and he did not die - (we know that life is eternal and there is no death). Judgement kills the creative expression – this is the only death there is.

As a vocal coach, Ann Meyer found that students who apologized and condemned themselves for each error, or criticized themselves, greatly impeded their progress, while those who simply corrected their mistakes, improved more rapidly. God called its creations "good and very good". It is a proven truth that what we praise grows and what we criticize tries it's best to disappear.

As we read further about the creation of Woman, we are told that Woman was created from the rib of a Man. The Man-Woman person was now divided into a man and a woman. Why? For the pleasure of relationship. We are both the giver and the receiver, given masculine and feminine functions to procreate. It is about the physical levels of creation.

Verse 25 reads "And the man and his wife were naked and unashamed." There was no need for shame in the minds of Man and Woman, for there was not yet any judgment resulting in fear or guilt. Originally, the sexual expression was simply an honest, natural expression, of desire and acceptance. Such an attitude can only produce healthy, happy living.

Rev. Ann stated that the Angels, or Beings on higher levels of vibration, freely read one another's thoughts, for they have no need to hide anything from one another. They exchange unjudging love. Only human beings, with their judgments, moral rules, fears, and guilt, feel the need to cover their thoughts, feelings, with pretense and their physical bodies with clothing.

In Genesis, Chapter Three, we learn of the subtle serpent, whom we shall call "Influence". Influence is the capacity to have an effect on the behavior or character of someone. Often, this is about impressing others rather than the purpose of self-expression. The serpent told the woman (the sub-conscious) that if she ate the apple, "You will not die, but your eyes will be open and you will be like God, knowing good from evil." This is self-deception – our only real enemy. Positive thinking without judgment can heal the ills of humanity. We must guard ourselves against the temptation of judgment and criticism and replace it with discernment - perception with a spiritual view.

Of course, as the story goes, the woman takes the apple and eats it. In Verse 7, she gives the apple to the man; He ate it and their eyes were opened, and they knew they were naked. They saw the differences between each other and clothed themselves with fig leaves. (Immediate - self rejection and the plague of the rejection of sex.) They hid themselves "among the trees" from their Creator. They created the idea of "<u>Separation</u>", which is the cause of illness, lack, difficulties and the troubles of the world. This is possibly the greatest lesson of this story.

Then, God called out to them, "Where are you?" All through the ages, this cry has come from the Creator to the Christ-Self of every human being. The human race, guilty and ashamed, believes in separation from God. When God saw that the humans had eaten the forbidden fruit, the man blamed the woman and the woman blamed the serpent. This was inevitable, as where there is judgment, there is blame. The man (intellect) blames the woman (emotions), and the woman (emotions) blames the serpent (temptation from outside the self).

The consequences are pain (as in childbirth, the result of sexual guilt). Pain or great internal struggle can also come as part of the creative process such as an invention, or a work of art. We were designed to have creative ideas and creative flow with ease and joy, but our resistance (judgment/guilt) creates the internal struggle. The results are that mankind thinks we must work hard for a living, endure with a sense of burden, and grapple with the illusion of a lack of time to really enjoy the fruits of our labors.

Hebrew mythology and rabbinic literature also tells another story of creation with Adam's first wife named Lilith, and Eve as his second wife. Shekhinah is the feminine aspect of Divinity, also referred to as the Divine Presence. This term appears in the Kabbalah.

The Islamic creation account, like the Hebrew one, involves **Adam and Eve** as the first parents, living in paradise. As in the Hebrew story, God warns **Adam and Eve** not to eat fruit from a certain tree, but they do anyway, earning expulsion from Paradise. This narrative is further developed in many verses in the Qur'an.

The Chinese philosophy of Taoism, established in the 6th Century BC, also professes the masculine and feminine in human nature which we most commonly recognize in the Yin-Yang symbol. These aspects are considered masculine and feminine and are defined as united and complimentary.

Somehow, although these philosophies have acknowledged the existence of the masculine and feminine natures within us, each have contributed to the internal judgment and self-doubt women have sustained and why we are still working on equality,

Sometimes women fear men or try to please men, seeking their favor. The bondage of women, which still happens all over the world, will end when humanity learns to balance the intuitive nature with the intellect and at last becomes the whole and happy human beings we were created to be.

Many women have found their rightful place and function in the world quite successfully. The more both men and women find this balance we will experience greater relationships for all humanity.

> *"Fear was born of a false idea of separation of man from man, of man from God. Through a sense of Oneness you will know your fears away. . . Meditate on this Oneness. If you will do this you shall grow out of all sense of fear and as your fear is eliminated there shall be for you nothing to fear.*
>
> "GOD'S WILL" - BROTHERHOOD OF THE FOLLOWERS OF THE PRESENT JESUS - 1965

The following affirmations include references to beauty. This is not about the art of being pretty or beautiful in your appearance. It is about the *quality* and *feeling* of beauty that comes from deep within, and permeates your actions, reactions and decisions.

Think of the first time you saw a spectacular waterfall, the magnificent Grand Canyon, massive ocean waves, the Giant Redwoods or other stunning gifts of nature. Recall the first look at a newborn baby. Think of the extraordinary effect of those breathtaking "firsts". This is the *experience* of beauty. In those moments you feel a degree of reverence. You inhale this beauty and exhale gratitude. You feel fully alive. This is the power of beauty. Not Madison Avenue beauty – *expressions of our Creator* beauty. That beauty is within you. It is the well-spring of life. This beauty connects us to life and to each other. Indeed, YOU have this beauty within.

I once sat on a beach on the island of Morea, in the South Pacific and gazed at the millions of stars that formed the Milky Way. I sat there in absolute awe and wonderment. It was at a low point in my life but the experience of that beauty connected me to peace, to hope and to a knowingness that I, although having no idea how to "fix" my circumstances, I could surrender my painful circumstances to the magnificent power that created the dazzling scene before me.

Lesson Two
Explanations of Affirmations

I AM ALL that Woman is. I possess every quality inherent in a Universal Woman. Nothing has been left out; I lack nothing that any other woman possesses. All I can imagine Perfect Universal Woman to be, I AM.

I am Beauty. I am not just beautiful, I _am_ beauty. I am a unique expression of the principle of beauty. (Pause to feel this beauty in your mind and body and enjoy it.)

I am Love. As Universal Woman, I am the Love Nature of God. I am an expression of Universal Love. All of God is Love, but I, as a woman, am the Feminine Love aspect of Love. I am created as the love nature of humankind.

I am tenderness and gentleness. Gain the feeling of these words as you say them. It will feel good.

I am warmth, I am softness. Softness is a characteristic of the body, mind and heart of a woman.

I am grace, and am perfect, ageless, woman form. Affirming this daily, will actually improve your physical form and the way you carry yourself. Women are naturally graceful, and can infuse grace in every situation. It is part of the feminine charm.

I am acceptance. Universal Woman is non-judging, and all accepting. As a woman, I accept God; I accept love; I accept my good; I accept man. There is no need for manipulations, which only come from fear-based thinking. Anything that I can truly accept on all levels of mind, I can have.

I am flexible. I accept change, and adjustments and do not resist my good. I am irresistible through loving acceptance.

I am receptive. I am receptive to Love. I am free to express love and receive love, wisely with whom I choose. I reject no one, and the Universal Woman within guides my choices.

I am responsiveness. I respond to love, completely and joyfully. The feminine vibration absolutely radiates from me. My personal magnetism draws more Love into my life.

Add these and the following affirmations to your daily Woman Awareness Meditations. Enjoy...

The Universal Woman Treatment
Lesson Two

I am all that Universal Woman is.

I am beauty.

I am Love.

I am tenderness and gentleness.

I am warmth.

I am grace.

I am perfect woman form.

I am acceptance.

I am flexibility.

I am receptivity.

I am responsiveness.

I am alluring, magnetic, irresistible Woman

I am as feminine as any woman who has ever lived.

I am loved and loving, desired and desiring, adored and adoring.

I am a free, perfect expression of Woman Love.

Notes

LESSON THREE

True Equality = Balance
The Equality of a Woman in a Male-Female World

GREETINGS AND PRAISE to you, wonderful woman created in the image of the feminine nature of God! If you have made a sincere effort to eliminate judgment and criticism of yourself and others from your mind, you are already seeing positive changes in your life. In this lesson, we will move forward in the greater realization of our divine freedom as an aware woman and true equality with man.

In the outer world, there are wide variances in appearance, intelligence, wealth, etc. No two persons are alike and fairness often appears impossible. It is in the inner world, in our spiritual being, where we are developing our awareness. <u>True equality exists in our inner worth</u> and inner resources, first. The Truth is that deep within every person is a beautiful, flawless soul. We are each given the opportunity for the realization of equality, and to manifest our inner wholeness in the outer world.

A woman's true sense of equality with a man is achieved through the equalization, integration or balance of the masculine and feminine natures of her own being.

Beyond basic needs lies desire. Desire and fulfillment are two aspects of a single idea. There is no desire which does not have within it the seed of its own fulfillment. It is a Universal Law. Rejection of desire is based on fear, doubt, guilt, or lack of worthiness.

Fulfillment comes when will and intellect connect with Love through the nature of the heart. Actions and decisions are empowered when sourced from the wholeness of our being. Balance is the key for co-creating with Spirit the life that you desire.

In a partnership or marriage, the aspects of the feminine and masculine natures may be balanced within the relationship or in each one's roles in the outer world. Our goal is for the masculine and feminine principles to become balanced within each woman.

Women have made great progress in the world, yet our culture has been functioning from the intellectual or masculine nature, while the feminine nature has still been considered weak, thus the continuation of war after war. We have seen many women "break glass ceilings" moving forward in the business world, many of whom have done so by embracing their masculine natures. Powerful women still must achieve balance within to advance all humankind.

Rev. Ann Meyer shares an example of balance through her experience of writing a play….

"One day, unexpectedly, I received a wonderful idea for a metaphysical play which I felt would be appropriate production for a Science of Mind church. At the time, all I received was the initial idea. I knew that it was good, and that soon, I would write the play. I then asked the minister for permission to produce this unwritten play, telling him with a laugh, 'I haven't written it yet, but I am going to write it.'

We scheduled the performance for an occasion, several months away. Soon after, I began to know the general format of the plot and the different characters. Then I fully cast the play, saying to each prospective actor, 'I haven't written the play yet, but I am going to write it.' They all accepted, and with the play completely cast, we planned the rehearsal dates.

The minister's wife, who was in charge of the program for the evening, asked me how long this play was going to be. Without hesitation, I replied, 'It will be thirty minutes long.' This was not a guess; somewhere in my mind was the knowledge of the exact length of my play.

As time for rehearsals drew near, I made plans for the writing of the play. It was a Tuesday, and I would be relaxed and spending several hours at a beauty salon. I took a writing pad and pencil with me, and before the day was over, I had written my play. Word by word, all dialog, action and scenes were in order, and not one word needed to be changed, nor order of scenes rearranged.

The play had a complicated plot, with five characters as five threads of the story being woven together and five separate personal problems reach their climaxes and woven together at the same moment, in perfect balance.

If I had fitted together this complicated five-fold plot with my intellect alone, I know that I would have been revising and polishing my play for weeks. Instead, I allowed my subconscious mind to put the play together in its entirety, and all I had to do was write it down, as though copying an already existing play.

The play turned out to be a successful presentation, and when we timed the final rehearsal, we found that the play was exactly thirty minutes long."

The idea for the play was the masculine principle, the formulating and writing of the play is the feminine principle. When creativity is in balance, results can be achieved with minimal effort and no fear. It just flows and falls into place.

> "Know that what you do in faith, trusting God for the action
> and the results, is done by the <u>Divine Presence</u> through you - is
> done by the hand of God, the mouth of God, the heart of God.
> Trust yourself <u>as the instrument</u> of this action of Spirit."
>
> <u>LOVE ANSWERS ALL</u> -BROTHERHOOD OF THE
> FOLLOWERS OF THE PRESENT JESUS – 1985

This is not "*magical thinking*" as it may appear - it is TRUST. Trust your Woman's insight for it is wise and sometimes even miraculous. You are actually trusting God. When you are willing to use the words, "*I of myself do nothing, it is the will of God that does it all*", you embrace the attitude of an *instrument* of God. You are trusting as a Christ being. Not wishing and hoping, but moving to a place beyond believing, to the place of KNOWING and ALLOWING.

How easy and effortless all creative action, all living, can be when the masculine and feminine aspects of our individual beings are working together in balance.

In the creation of a human child, the man really has very little to do. He merely assists in the conception and the time required for this is only a few moments. The woman spends nine months fulfilling her part of the action. The implanted seed takes form, is nourished, grows and is prepared for birth in the hidden regions of the woman's body. It is the same with all creative endeavors. The idea is prepared for production in the hidden realm of the sub-conscious mind.

In this world we all work too hard. If we learn to use the conscious and sub-conscious aspects of our minds in perfect balance, living can become a natural flow and our creative expressions quite simple and most glorious.

The Feminine Principle as Woman is the Love nature, the feeling nature, with the power of the subconscious mind. The Masculine Principle as Man is the leader and decider, but The Feminine Principle is the Power. Knowing this brings through greater excitement in the sexual expression. To be clear, this does not mean that women are to be subjective to men and allow men to make decisions for her. A woman may function in her everyday life as a balanced whole person. Women have taken leadership roles in work, business, world affairs, etc., and to experience these roles as fulfillment, it is important to become aware of these balance issues.

Observing the world as it is right now, it is easy to take issue with the Male aspect, and its aggressive behaviors. We seem to be at war, endlessly. We have a US Department of War. In the past **236 years** we have been fighting in some type of conflict **for 214 years or** about 90% of the time. It often appears completely out of balance, but when both the Male and Female aspect are balanced within each of us, we can co-create a new path for ourselves and for the world. We can create paths to peace, perhaps a Department for Peace.

What can happen is that when you are aware of both aspects within yourself and you find that you are confronted with a situation that appears or feels difficult, look within and determine whether you are operating from a masculine or feminine principle. Find the balancing principle and shift into that. Watch the dynamics of the situation change.

Working Mother magazine issued an article titled "The World's 50 Most Successful Moms 2017". Helle Thorning Schmidt, (Listed as #3 of 50) formerly the first female Prime Minister of Denmark, is now the CEO of Save the Children International which promotes the rights of children worldwide.

(Save the Children was founded in 1919, in London, England by sisters, Eglantyne Jebb and Dorothy Buxton, to alleviate the starvation of children after the effects of World War I. Millions of children have been aided through the efforts of this organization as the world continues to create wars as an answer to who is in power.)

Helle has called for a European solution for the [war] refugee crisis explaining that half of the refugees in need of help are children. She has attributed some of her success to conflict preparedness. "You should never be afraid of a fight. If you aren't ready for it you'll be surprised by it," she said.

In this woman we find a great example of balance between the masculine and feminine aspects that has gained world-wide achievement and recognition. Her feminine instincts drive her and the understanding and balanced use of her masculine aspects have empowered her success. What she terms "preparedness" is a conscious awareness and use of both aspects of her being and the courage to step forward. She trusts that this will bring the desired results.

In a conscious relationship the Feminine Aspect has the power to inspire and magnetize the Masculine Aspect of desire.
    The Masculine desire takes the initiative toward the expression of Love.
    The Feminine responds, through free choice.
    The Masculine expresses a desire - The Feminine accepts.
    The Masculine desires the action - The Feminine is the Power.
    In your new awareness, you will find this energy as the dance of life.

I would like to add another story, which happened to me while writing this book. I had been working at ways to identify the masculine/feminine aspects within myself and to be more conscious of the shifting of one to another in areas of problem solving. This was my experience…and it all happened in a matter of minutes.
    While at a stop sign at a busy intersection on my way to work one morning, I noticed a little gray cockapoo dog literally prancing down the sidewalk on the other side of the street, obviously reveling in its freedom.
    Since there were no cars behind me, I waited at the intersection and watched the little dog. I knew this was a little "escaped runaway" out on an adventure. I decided that when the traffic cleared, I would cross the road, pick up this little sweetie and try to help find its home.
    All of a sudden, in the blink of an eye, the little dog decided to cross the street and stepped out into the traffic. One, two, three cars zoomed right passed and then he stopped right in the middle of the street. A fourth car ran right over the little dog and just kept right on going.
    Immediately, I got out of my car and went to the little lifeless body. A van coming from the other direction stopped and a beautiful young man got out and joined me. More cars just slowed down and went around us. He asked me what had happened. I shared the chain of events and after a brief moment we both agreed that the little dog was indeed dead.
    I was stunned by it all and my emotions were inwardly raging from anger at the car that hit this pup, to sadness over this needless death. I knew what needed

to be done, and done quickly, but I was "emotionally stuck" in the shock and melancholy of what I had just witnessed.

The handsome young man groaned in sadness, yet quickly found the number for Animal Control. He asked me if I was okay to make the call to Animal Control, as he did not want to be late for his job.

I agreed, pulled myself together and made the call. I shared my concern as to children possibly walking about in search of their missing dog and seeing this disaster. The young woman on the phone seemed emotional over this too, and they came right over.

I got in my car and said a blessing for the soul of little dog and also a blessing of gratitude for the young man who stopped to help.

As I drove onto the freeway, I found myself taking a hard look at what had happened from a different perspective.

I knew that FEAR had stopped me from jumping out of my car and attempting to stop traffic to get the little dog out of the intersection. Shock kept me frozen as I witnessed the violent death of the dog. Then GUILT set in. I *would have – could have – should have* done this differently. Whoopee! I am supposed to be writing a book on balancing the masculine/feminine aspects. I felt weak – I failed. No balance there!

Here's what I learned…

Judgement and self-criticism were my adversary.

My intentions to retrieve the dog and take it to a safe place – Balanced.

Discernment led me to decide not to walk through the busy intersection – Balanced.

When the dog was hit - my response to was both fearless and compassionate – Balanced.

The young man who stopped to help was emotional and action oriented – Balanced.

I was stuck and got unstuck and made the call for help – Balanced

I took charge without regard of fear of further oncoming traffic - Balanced.

Said a blessing for the little dog and a prayer of gratitude for the young man. – Balanced

I proceeded with my day and did not speak of it until much later in the day, with a Prayer Partner. I realized that my own self-criticism and judgement is the very thing that has held me back - over and over in my lifetime.

How could I expect to be treated as an equal when I am so judgmental of myself? Fear and self-criticism are exactly why we are not treated as equals. This is the adversary we must conquer.

> *"We have propelled ourselves through many fears in our progress upward. You shall meet many new fears. But look through them to the idea within. As you do this you may love your fears. You may walk into them without struggle. You may tune in to the new joy and peace which shines from the midst of them. ... For peace surrounds your fear and is within it, so be at peace."*
>
> EVERLASTING PEACE - BROTHERHOOD OF THE
> FOLLOWERS OF THE PRESENT JESUS - 1966

Universal Woman Treatment 3

I know everything a Universal Woman knows. I am balanced and whole.

Feminine Intelligence within me is constantly revealing new truths about the feminine aspect of my true nature. I call forth the Masculine aspect of myself as needed.

I know that I am a completely fulfilled woman. All my needs are met and desires are gloriously fulfilled.

All necessary circumstances and experiences are perfectly created for me by the Law of my Being, which manifests a perfect partner for me, now.

These words set into motion Universal Laws that cannot be denied and therefore manifest according to consciousness –

(Instantaneously, if you are willing)

The Spiritual Feminist

Relationship Equality Meditation

This meditation can be used as a healing tool in any relationship.

Simply enter the name of your partner in the blanks

I am a whole, balanced person of great value, and worthy of every effort for relationship.
I have happiness and fulfillment to share.
My Spirit is a treasure.
My mind is a treasure.
My body is a treasure.
I am precious beyond measure.
I am a treasure for _____ and _____ is a treasure for me.
My partner is of great value to me, and worthy of every effort for relationship.
_____ contributes to my happiness and fulfillment.
_____ Spirit is a treasure for my Spirit.
_____ mind is a treasure for my mind.
_____ body is a treasure for my body.
_____ is precious beyond measure.
_____ is a treasure for me and I am a treasure for _____.

This meditation can neutralize our judgements, and adjust our attitudes about our partner, or a specific person, with whom we may be in relationship. Practice this meditation and watch the dynamic of conflict/resolution change dramatically.

The following is Rev. Ann Meyer's original Man-Woman Relationship Meditation.........

The Man-Woman Meditation

*This meditation can be used as a healing tool in any relationship.
Simply substitute the name of your partner, for the word Man.*

You may also use a particular man's name in place of the word "Man". This meditation can neutralize our judgements, and adjust our attitudes about men in general or a specific man, with whom we may be in relationship. Practice this meditation and watch the dynamic of conflict/resolution change dramatically.

The short meditation below held great value to Rev. Ann. She carried it around on a card for several years and used it when she felt of little value as a woman. She writes *"The card on which written was tear-stained, for I often wept over it, as I read it aloud – It seemed impossibly untrue to me. However, it helped to change my belief about myself and my relationship to men."* It goes like this....

>I am a treasure for Man.
>I am of great value to Man, and worthy of every effort for relationship
>I have happiness and fulfillment to give to Man.
>My Spirit is a treasure for Man's Spirit.
>My mind is a treasure for Man's mind.
>My body is a treasure for Man's body.
>I am a "Pearl of Great Price" for Man.
>I am precious beyond measure.
>I am a treasure for Man and Man is a treasure for me.
>
>Man is a treasure for me.
>Man is of great value to me, and worthy of every effort for relationship
>Man has happiness and fulfillment to give to me.
>Man's Spirit is a treasure for my Spirit.
>Man's mind is a treasure for my mind.
>Man's body is a treasure for my body.
>Man is a "Pearl of Great Price"* for me.

Man is precious beyond measure.
Man is a treasure for me and I am a treasure for Man.

*Matthew 13: 45-46 (A reference to Heaven) *"Who, when he had found one pearl of great price, went and sold all that he had, and bought it."*

Relationships can be complicated, and during the week of this spiritual practice, issues may arise that you may want to discuss with your minister, a prayer partner, or a therapist. The surfacing of these issues is not negative but conversely positively presenting your readiness to release these issues and move into balance – forever! We always advise that you take everything into prayer.

Notes

LESSON FOUR

Polarity and a Sense of Worth

"You do not have to prove yourself - You have to know yourself."

– Rev. Ann Meyer

IT IS CONSCIOUSNESS that speaks. No matter what words we use to express our thoughts and feelings, our consciousness always speaks louder than our words. Our consciousness is what we are. Our consciousness is what other people are really seeing when they look at us. This realization came to Rev. Ann when she attended her mother's funeral, noting that the physical body in the casket did not look like her mother at all. I had the exact same experience at my father's funeral. Who we had always seen was the essence of our parents, rather than their physical features.

We must realize that our consciousness includes both our conscious and subconscious levels of mind. The beliefs we have about ourselves, buried deep within the subconscious, plus the ideas we hold in our conscious minds, combine to form the concepts which are the laws that create our personal expressions and experiences.

A female student once told Rev. Ann that she would never be able to attract a man in her life. She had undergone a mastectomy and felt that she had become undesirable to men. This spoke to both her belief about herself and her beliefs about men. Rev. Ann Meyer told her of another woman she knew, who had for many years endured cerebral palsy. If one only looked at the physical appearance, she would have appeared misshapen, and trembling. She had difficulty with speech and with prolonged effort, spoke one word at a time. Yet, she had the consciousness of friendliness, attractiveness, and beauty. Her home was filled with friends and she was never without a man. <u>It is consciousness that speaks. We are as beautiful and attractive as we know ourselves to be.</u>

Today, you are the person you have affirmed with your thoughts and beliefs about yourself. If you desire to *become* more of your authentic self then you may affirm truths that generates that which you desire. Saying your affirmations builds consciousness. It is a process that will alter your beliefs systems. You are required to be diligent, and to incorporate your feeling nature as it is key to your best results. It is when both your thoughts (Mind) and feelings (Heart) are synchronized that you can co-create your own transformation. It is not that you are creating a *new* person – you are co-creating the *realization of your truth*.

Let us pursue the idea of a woman's true worth within the Masculine/Feminine Law of Polarity. Every individual idea is both masculine and feminine, for there are two sides to everything.

Polarity is about the circuitry of power. If there is a situation in your life, where you feel "stuck", look at where you may shift your perspective from masculine to feminine or vice versa.

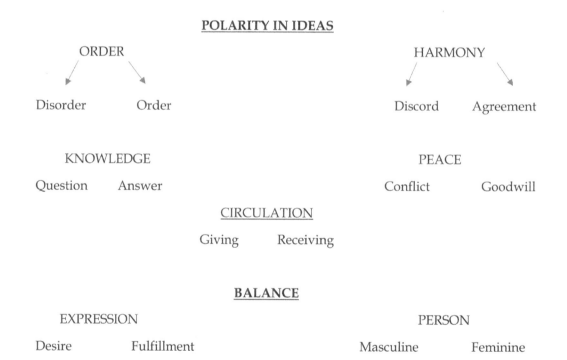

For example, let's say it is a housekeeping day and you like the idea of "Perfect Order". In our chart, ORDER includes disorder and order – two sides of the idea. You may need to move the furniture (disorder) to clean the floor, bringing the satisfaction of better order. Another example is a work desk. To perform the work tasks on the job, you may have to refer to several files on your desk all at once. (Disorder) The phone rings, you are asked a question that requires files opened and paperwork all over your desk. (More disorder – discord) You answer the question. (Order and agreement) The files are closed and put away. You now have ORDER (Masculine) and HARMONY (Feminine) within, which equals BALANCE.

When speaking of HARMONY, we most often think of music. Every musical composition is comprised of chords and discords. This is necessary for the feeling of action, direction and accomplishment. Without Harmony, which is integral to BALANCE, any composition (or creativity) would be incomplete.

We have no grasp of perfect KNOWLEDGE except through questions and answers.

Within PEACE is both rest and unrest, with unrest being the movement of growth into a new area of peace. Without periods of unrest, we would not grow or expand, and without growth and expansion, there would soon be no peace at all.

CIRCULATION is the activity of giving and receiving.

The key is to achieve BALANCE. Balancing the masculine and feminine aspects of being. <u>That balance within…expresses balance in our outer world.</u>

The Life EXPRESSION is composed of desire and fulfillment. Within each PERSON is the aspects of the masculine and feminine.

The masculine aspect of an idea or dilemma is the aggression or <u>unrest</u> part of the equation, the female aspect is the <u>rest or fulfillment.</u>

<u>Feminine Principle</u>	<u>Masculine Principle</u>
<u>Woman is the answer</u>	<u>to Man's question</u>
Order	Disorder
Harmony	Discord
Peace	Unrest
Fulfillment	Desire

PRAYER

Even prayer has both aspects. Speaking a prayer or affirmations aloud, is a masculine activity. Meditation, is listening, which is a feminine aspect of prayer.

Channeling is receiving and is therefore a feminine aspect as is a prayer of Surrender to God, (Thy Will be done).

In Matthew 26: 36-46, and Luke 22: 39-46, Jesus prayed in the Garden of Gethsemane, shortly before his arrest and trial. At first, he asks in anguish that "this cup be taken from me", (masculine aspect) but this prayer seemed to conflict with his deepest desires. To fulfill his life's mission and purpose, he surrendered his own will, (the feminine aspect) and prayed "Nevertheless, not as I will, but as Thy will be done" and he proceeded to leave the world with a lasting demonstration and proof of immortality.

For effective prayer, as for effective living, we need to have a combination of both the masculine and feminine polarities of activity. We need, through the intellect of the male aspect, to define clearly for what we are praying, and then in true femininity, surrender this desire to the highest will of God. Returning to the masculine aspect, we follow our prayer with inspired action. True prayer always inspires correct action.

This is the excitement and glory of polarity. Within each idea are both aspects, incomplete without the other. Have you ever been with a group of women and suddenly a man walks in, and the conversation changes?

Several years ago, my business operated with an all-female staff. During the Christmas holiday season, I usually took everyone out for a dinner and an event. One particularly prosperous year, I took the staff and also included their husbands. We had a completely different experience than in previous years. There was certainly nothing wrong with the evening, but at the next staff meeting we voted to keep the holiday event for the women only.

Again, we have both the masculine and feminine aspects as a whole person, and within the whole human race. We have proven the ability to function in what we used to call a "Man's World". That was *once upon a time* and women today, have discredited the myth. We function in roles as wives, mothers, sweethearts, along with business, civic, and world leadership. It can be exhausting but we are doing it.

Again, the key is BALANCE and for that you must value yourself as a whole person and take the steps necessary for fulfillment along with self-care. You do not have to prove yourself. You have to know yourself. God has provided you with a dual nature and will co-create with you for the fulfillment of your desires and divine purpose. It is time to stop being motivated by a sense of need, but to be motivated by a sense of worth. **You are important to all of humanity.**

"Dip into your own fountain; let Spirit flow through you. It is crystal pure clear Spirit, always waiting to flow. All you need do is ask and trust, and know the Spirit which is within you."

DAWNING OF THE AGE OF LIGHT – FOLLOWERS
OF THE PRESENT JESUS - 1979

Please add the following affirmations to your list. Say them with conviction.

Explanations of Affirmations – Lesson Four

I have all that the "collective woman" has. You can create every wonderful quality that is expressed by any other woman in the world. Think of the woman you admire the most in the world, and affirm that you have within your own being the same qualities.

I have an infinite amount of Universal Love. My love and desires are unlimited. I have no fear of my sexual desires. I find a healthy way to express and fulfill my desires. Through prayer, all my desires will be fulfilled.

"I have confidence in myself because I have confidence in God. I am sure of myself because I am sure of God."

JAMES WILLIS, RScP

Notes

LESSON FIVE

Universal Woman
Desire and Your Physical Health

"Abundance and fulfillment, are not about quantity but about quality."

REV. DAVID OWEN RITZ, AUTHOR OF KEYS TO THE KINGDOM

LET US BEGIN with a statement of Truth: "We Are Innately Perfect". We are created in the image of God - Universal Perfection – So how could we possibly be otherwise? We may understand the elements of perfection to be Divine order, love, intelligence, good, etc. These and many more ideas are included in the one idea of perfection.

Now, let us consider another very important element of perfection – The Fulfillment of Desire. We could not conceive of an all-loving, all-powerful intelligence, which could not and would not fulfill all of its desires instantly, and constantly. Therefore, it follows that we could not *truthfully* imagine this Divine Intelligence as not being ready at all times to fulfill a desire, everywhere.

However, what we experience may seem to be otherwise. What we experience is a reflection of our consciousness and what we value. If you believe you are unworthy of companionship, financial security or happiness, it will be immediately reflected in your life experiences. These lessons are to turn the focus of your worthiness toward love, joy, health, beauty and great relationships. Let the Universe reflect that.

Women must stop asking themselves "What's wrong with me?"

Every activity in life begins with desire. Desire is the only true cause, the source of every activity and every expression. *I am thirsty – I want a drink of water.* It is as simple as that. God, as perfect love, does not coerce or force action from anyone. This is a universe of choice. We create our lives through our own personal choices.

One Saturday afternoon, I was cleaning my house while listening to a broadcast from the Metropolitan Opera. I neither speak the languages nor know all the story lines, but have always been fascinated by the qualities of the operatic voice. My family does not appreciate the opera and, at that time a two hundred dollar opera ticket was not in my budget. *God knows I love classical entertainment*, I thought while polishing the bedroom furniture, so I stopped and said a prayer... *"Dear God, please find a way for me to attend the opera, the ballet, and the symphony – at least once. Thank you, Amen."* This was certainly not an eloquent prayer, just a simple request.

About two weeks later, with the request nearly forgotten, I received a call from a friend stating that a terrible flood had happened in his friend Bill's home. Bill was overwhelmed as to how to put the house back in order - Would I help? Of course I would. I called and set up an appointment to go to his house to view the damage. The insurance company had done a great job of cleaning up and they were simply waiting for Bill to choose new paint, flooring, fabrics, etc. Some furnishings needed to be refinished and works of art restored.

Six weeks later, when the restoration had been completed, I met with Bill for what I thought would be the last time to review the work and related invoices. He had been a pleasure to work with and was most appreciative. As I was about to leave, Bill thanked me again, then said, *"I would like you to consider something. I have season tickets to everything....the opera, ballet, symphony, and theater and would enjoy your company."*

Over the following fifteen years, I attended several operas, saw exquisite ballet companies from around the world, superb musical performances, hilarious theatrical plays, and formed a friendship with this wise world traveler and compassionate philanthropist. Each event was preceded by fine dining and a discussion that solved all the world's problems.

God had answered my little prayer "tamped down and overflowing" abundantly.

A simple request was all it took. A simple request given to the Creator and released to the Power of the Universe. And so it was – Desire fulfilled - Amen to that!

True individual choice is a blending of desire on levels of Spirit, soul and mind which embraces the whole human being. We teach that the choices of the human being originate with the I AM Self, and radiate outward through the Christ Self, the Soul, and resonate to the human personality as intuitive callings, talents, and natural interests. When we ignore these callings, we block the lines of desire and it deeply affects our overall well-being and health.

Often women try with the best of intentions to block this desire line, imagining (or judging) that it might not be "right" or "good". A true desire is always good for us, always right, even if it does not seem to fit in the current framework of our lives. True desire is the beginning of creativity, and is embedded in the soul. It is often referred to as your Life Purpose. Through prayer and meditation, guidance for the expression of your true desires will bring you to the highest expression of your true self.

The goal is fulfillment and it may come instantaneously, or it can take years, depending on your willingness, determination, and acceptance. The path to fulfillment can be littered with confusion, despair, and repression. You can construct barricades to fulfillment with fear, guilt, or self-condemnation. Simply the thought "*I am not enough*" can lead you down the path to depression and defeat.

All women must set aside cultural thinking and not let society determine your values. Your heart may say differently. The wisdom of your heart, through the nature of love, will guide you to the fullest expression of all that you are and all you desire to become.

A heroic example is Pakistani teenager Malala Yousafzai, who was shot in the head by the Taliban in 2012 for advocating girls' rights to education. In 2014, at 16 years of age, Malala won the Nobel Peace Prize, for as soon as she recovered from her wounds, she continued her campaign.

In 1979, Mother Teresa, at the age of 69, won the Nobel Peace Prize. She gave her desire to God in her prayers, which was "*Make me your instrument, nothing more.*" Her accomplishments are legendary.

The principle presented here is that it is our nature to be motivated by desire and we cannot be successful by going against our own feminine nature.

For centuries society was successful at molding women into roles through suppression. To be the "good" woman, we went along with it.

Many women today don't realize that women have only had the right to vote for less than one hundred years. (Since 1920) The desire for Women's Rights were "fought for" and although successful, a great deal of anger and violence resulted.

A small, core peace movement had long existed in the United States, largely based in Quaker and Unitarian beliefs. At the time the Woman Awareness book was first published the Anti-War Movement had built a strong nationwide grassroots organization, motivated by the desire for peace, yet it too was torn with anger and violence.

At the same time in 1968, ground-breaking TV shows such as "That Girl" showed women with ideas and a voice in the workplace. "Mission Impossible" had a female member of a team of government spies. "Peyton Place", produced after a successful novel and film, created sensational weekly episodes with sexually oppressed women who began to take charge and fulfill their desires.

The Woman Awareness book was written to liberate repressed sexual expressions and to incorporate – not separate them from women's spiritual expressions. Today, we often hear the expression *"Love is Love"* when addressing sexuality. Let's give Rev. Ann credit for planting that seed with every one of her students.

What does all of this have to do with Physical Health and Beauty? It is about expression as opposed to repression. What happens to your body when inhibited desires silence your calling or conceal your truth?

Let us consider a few physical disorders which can be caused by the repression of sexual desires or personal expressions and how we may remedy these difficulties.

The Awkward Stage…. so called, results when a young woman, because of the teachings of her childhood, is reaching puberty and is trying to grow into womanhood, while trying not to grow up. She may unconsciously try to remain a sexless form, to be the "good girl", for her family, while television, films and music tell her otherwise. If the focus is on building her confidence and inner harmony, she will transform from "good girl" to "Good at being a Girl".

Menstrual Difficulties… Rev. Ann wrote: I believe these difficulties result from conscious or unconscious reject of the birth cycle which is continuous all through the month in women's bodies. Many girls are taught while quite young that menstruation is a bother, something to be endured, hidden, and not talked about. (Especially with boys and men). This wonderful function has been given nicknames such as "the curse". We can imagine how the subconscious mind responds to this. [Thus the entire PMS syndrome, which has created huge product lines for the consumption of young women.]

Instead, we must teach young girls to give thanks to God for being a woman, with the capacity to create another human being. I thank God for the healthful benefits of this continuously creative activity. Even if a woman chooses not to have children, then she may thank God, she is not pregnant.

Rev. Ann further stated …"*many women who have chosen to follow this line of thinking have eliminated their own menstrual difficulties.*"

<u>Menopause</u> … Rev. Ann wrote: Early or troublesome menopausal symptoms may be the result of self-rejection and the woman nature. She stated, "*Some years ago, I went through menopause, then discovered the Woman Awareness ideas, which completely changed my life. One of the totally unexpected results of completing my daily affirmations, was that suddenly my menstrual periods resumed and were fuller more regular than ever before in my life. Several other women have had the same results.*"

Could it be that menopause and possibly all aging processes, are caused by self-rejection, or habitual thoughts over a long period of time, of the feminine nature? Scientists are predicting that fertility rates will continue to be prolonged in the future. Women are now having babies in their fifties. Could this be longer youth due to greater self-acceptance?

<u>Painful childbirth</u> … The return to natural childbirth has been consistently progressing for decades. Pain is tension caused by fear. Fear causes resistance which obstructs the natural processes of birth. We must openly praise the birth process right from the beginning of a pregnancy, so no resistance is built up in the mind. Most mothers can now claim exhilaration at the moment of birth with tears of joy.

<u>Infections of the Female Organs</u> … is most often the result of anger, regarding either sexual rejection or anger toward a past or present mate, which can be dissolved through prayer, treatment and meditation. Chronic infections must be treated, as with the chronic beliefs, either current or longstanding.

<u>Obesity</u> … There are many causes for the obesity epidemic in the United States. For the purpose of this study, we believe it may be linked to lack of unexpressed love, both inwardly as self-love and outwardly as loving others. Sometimes sexual repression is at the root of this health issue. When sexual expression is not satisfied it may be redirected toward children as excessive maternal love, or upon the partner. (Often through food.) This type of distortion may create a ponderous maternal type of figure. Such maternal women often refer to their husbands as "Daddy", like being addressed as "Mommy" and have sweet pet names for their children.

It is imperative that you treat any physical manifestation mentally, physically, emotionally and spiritually. There is no *one cause* and no *one cure*, it is all consciousness. Until we have thoroughly cleansed all negative beliefs, all environmental toxins, all food contamination, all hatred, all discrimination from humankind, we will continue to see imbalances in health, wealth and relationships.

The truth is… all you can do is create your own love life and the best way to begin that is to love God. Many master teachers have told us that we are loved far more than we can even comprehend. Can we start there? Can we know that we are a creative expression of Life, and that alone should make us healthy and beautiful?

Prayer for the realization of perfect health...

I know that God is the one magnificent Power and Presence, that created, operates and maintains, this incredibly beautiful and ever-expanding universe; with galaxies and stars; and planets and moons; the sun and all things seen and unseen in between… And Life – It is All Life – and I AM LIFE, and in my Oneness with God and All of Life, I find Holiness.

In that place of Holiness, I can achieve anything, as I co-create with the Holy Spirit for my highest good and the good of others.

I give thanks for Divine Order in and Balance in this Universe, on this Earth, and in me – in my body, in my mind, and in the body of my affairs. In that highest good – I give thanks for Divine Wisdom that guides my decisions and actions.

I give thanks for eyes that see the beauty that surrounds me, the beauty in others, and the beauty in myself.

I give thanks for the ability to hear the gentle whispers of Divine Guidance, the ability to understand them, and the courage to act upon them.

I give thanks for the ability to speak and write loving words of wisdom and grace.

I give thanks for Christ Love that fills my heart, overflows and reaches out to all those that I meet today.

I give thanks as that same Christ Love overflows into each and every cell of my body, meeting the Life Force of God that already exists in every cell of my body. Together they meet and burst into Light and I AM a Being of Light. That Light cleanses me, heals me, and releases from me, anything less than wholeness and vitality.

It generates for me……

Shiny, lustrous beautiful hair

Creamy, smooth and absolutely flawless skin

Eyes that see with Love, and are formed for 20/20 vision

Finely tuned hearing, taste, touch and smell.

Pure free lungs that breathe Breath of Life - circulating healing oxygen throughout my body and into my brain; particularly stimulating areas of creativity.

My heart beats rhythmically, strongly, coursing perfectly balanced red cell/white cell, rich blood through clean, clear arterial walls and veins.

All internal systems harmonized.
All hormonal systems balanced.
I AM LIFE, expressing as a woman, named _____. I am God's Woman, Pure Woman, and all that Woman is. I AM the Essence of Femininity.
I humbly, and lovingly give thanks, knowing that these words, set into motion God's Universal Laws that cannot be denied and therefore, must manifest.
In the name and nature of a Christ, that lives within me.
Amen – And so it is.

I said this prayer every morning during a difficult time of a major health challenge and cured, what was once thought incurable. *The Life Force of God lives in every cell of my body* is a very powerful statement and for me – it worked. The realization of that truth came to me after seeing a film of a single blood cell under a microscope. In a single cell you will see the membrane, nucleus and several other minute particles circulating within the cell. When asked what is in between each of these particles that allowed them such activity, the doctor answered, "the life force". The Life Force? The film continued but I was stopped in thought. The Life Force is God - breathing me, making my heart beat, etc., etc. It is energy and light. If this exists in every cell of my body – why would we ever get sick? So I've used that affirmation since 2004.

Any part of the human body can be a focus in this prayer. I once had a young woman share with me her experience of extreme hormonal issues, and other problems with female organs. We spoke a great length about her ability to realize a healing through loving and praising her ovaries, uterus, etc., and gave her some affirmations. Two weeks later, she had cut her medications in half and was noticing quite an amazing difference. This young woman dressed casually and usually wore jeans and a shirt to church. The next Sunday, she had on a lovely skirt and blouse. She said, *"I'm feeling much better and for some reason felt like wearing something a little more feminine today."* She knew nothing about this book, but certainly felt the power of the feminine force within her.

The first time I drove up the West Coast into the Pacific Northwest, I was completely enchanted by the lush green landscapes and the towering trees. My first thoughts about it were, *Mother Nature has surely been busy up here!* As women, we can say we are aligned with that same feminine nature. In the Pacific

Northwest, we can physically see, touch and feel an abundant, creative force in the magnificent wealth of plants, flowers and trees, lovingly nourished by all the rain they need. It is a wonderful example of Divine Abundance.

So, in addition to your health – you may add to your affirmations…

I AM a direct descendant of Mother Nature herself, constantly creating from amazing abundance and limitless prosperity!

Add these affirmations to your list…………

Explanations of Affirmations - Lesson Five

I am a sensual woman. With love, I praise my womanly body – its sexual organs, its reproductive and hormonal systems. As I send this love and praise, I maintain my health, and increase my feelings of joy and desire.

I give thanks to God for the ability to see the beauty that surrounds me, the beauty in others and the beauty in myself. Take a few seconds when you greet each person that you meet today and see the beauty that exists in them. Know that what you are truly seeing is not just the beauty in them, but a reflection of the beauty within yourself.

Note: Be prepared to come alive in new ways. Aside from increased sexual fulfillment, these affirmations can balance your hormones, resulting in an easier pregnancy, balanced monthly cycles, and symptom free menopause. Amen to that!

Notes

LESSON SIX

Universal Woman
The Creative Principle and Sexuality

"Sexuality can be a profound demonstration of your love, and especially your freedom, to express and bond. Spiritual sex, then, combines how you express your love with the intentions or blessings you bring to your partnership."

ALEXANDRA KATEHAKIS, AUTHOR

CREATION IS THE eternal and constant action of God. The Universe is always in a state of expansion, and something is always being created through the masculine-feminine principle of creation as explained in previous lessons.

Let us consider the following as the creative expression....

WILL	LAW		
Masculine Aspect	Feminine Aspect	=	Creative Expression
ASSERTIVENESS	RECEPTIVITY	→	EXPERIENCE
OBJECTIVITY	SUBJECTIVITY		

The Will of God, of Life, or of a human being, acting through Love, (the Law) creates form. Will, asserts itself, while the Law is receptive, resulting in a creative expression. The Will is objective, (the Masculine aspect), the Law (Love) is subjective (Feminine aspect) and together creates an experience. This is a Principle of Polarity.

As human beings, we are made in the image of the Divine, and are composed of both aspects of being. Each person, may express both the masculine and feminine aspects of being. When a woman is teaching a class, she is asserting her knowledge, and is in her masculine aspect and the students, as receivers, are in the feminine aspect. The students will have a greater experience of the class by staying receptive, and without judgment until after the class.

Likewise, writing a message is a masculine assertion, while reading the message is feminine. Speaking your mind, is the masculine aspect, while listening, the feminine.

Sex is the creative principle expressing constantly through every action of life. Sex is Life energy expressing on all levels. In pure God Thought there is neither high nor low. The physical vibration is as dear to God as the etheric and Christ levels. We are placed on earth to be happy on earth – to enjoy ourselves and each other. For the realization of the beauty and wonder of the sex principle, we must release judgments, bondages, shame and race-mind thinking and express freely from our love nature. Our whole expression of Life can be freed.

A pleasurable sexual relationship is a lot like the American Tango, which has evolved as an unjudged social dance with an emphasis on leading and following skills. It has a creative, balancing rhythm of the male and female aspects of polarity. It is considered a most sensual dance as it is a partner dance that is characterized by a very close embrace, small steps, and syncopated rhythmic actions.

The real secret of femininity is to relax all judgment of sexual expression. Let it be an expression of Love and enjoyment. Do not judge your partner or yourself – just enjoy. By constantly affirming that your sexual expression is perfect, your partner is perfect, you are perfect – there is greater satisfaction and pleasure for both of you.

Judgment is the greatest block to fulfillment, which is true in every area of your life. Let go of the "Yes, but…" mentality and watch your life change. It is incredibly liberating not to have an opinion (judgment) about everything or everyone else. Nobody died and left you in charge of how someone else lives their life. You may be surprised how much more energy you will have by releasing judgment and giving praise. This is truly a feminine aspect of Universal Woman.

Rev. Ann Meyer stated that, *"Dissolving judgment is the shortest route to perfecting any technique. I proved this for myself in my own singing technique. The day I resolved to never again judge my public appearances marked the beginning of great, continuing improvements in my singing techniques. Naturally, I continued to practice faithfully, employing self-honesty and discernment, but once I had sung a song in public, I immediately released it from my mind. It was finished, unjudged, enjoyed and given to God as my best, and perfect for now.*

The surprising result was that I began to be perfectly relaxed while singing in public. Indeed, my technique was completely at my command and I concentrated not upon listening to myself, but solely on communicating with my audience. Our minds cannot concentrate on two ideas at the same instant. If we allow ourselves to wonder how we are doing, we cannot concentrate on expressing ourselves. To quote some of my Woman Awareness students, 'You can create paralysis with analysis.'"

Sexual love is a spontaneous creative expression, always new, different every time, both a mental and physical expression. Love-making requires complete concentration. Let go of your day, your problems or concerns, and surrender to the pure pleasure of the loving exchange. Focus on being receptive and stay in the feminine mind. In this state you can fully express the pleasure and passion of sexual love.

How can we ever know what the future will bring, or how we and our desires may change, as we grow in consciousness? When living a prayerful life, doing our best, we can always depend on the future to be better than the now.

Rev. Ann Meyer states: *"I see the whole human race as swimming about in an ocean of Love. By the Law of Attraction, some swim together and by the same Law, some may swim apart, but they are always surrounded by Love."*

The Feminine Aspect has the power to inspire and magnetize the Masculine Aspect of desire.

The Masculine desire takes the initiative toward the expression of Love.

The Feminine responds, with free choice.

The Masculine directs the action the Feminine is the Power.

The Masculine expresses and the Feminine accepts.

This appears in the sexual expression, and also in the dance of life.

In your new awareness, you will find the energy of this dance purely enjoyable.

Making Love is a marvelous way to relieve stress. Give Love with every bit of your mind, emotions, and body. Let Love's wisdom direct the giving. This is true femininity.

This chapter is to address and encourage sexual freedoms of consenting adults. At no time is sexual abuse of any kind acceptable. Sexual freedoms are meant to be a pleasurable act of love between consenting adults. In many ways worldwide, our society and other cultures have sexualized children. We, as compassionate Universal Women, cannot ignore this and must help these young girls heal. We must create greater ways to protect them, educate them and honor them.

Explanation of Affirmations – Lesson Six

I know all that Universal Woman knows for perfect sexual expression. We already possess in our natures, all the knowledge necessary for our perfect sexual expression. Each one of us naturally knows far more than any instructions in any book, or advice from any sex expert. It requires only one person's opening to greater awareness to improve any relationship.

I release any false barriers which block the flow of my innate, intuitive knowledge. As we make the leap from understanding to knowing, we begin to express marvelously and naturally. Knowing the truth for one's self and for your partner, the partner is also freed for greater self-expression.

I AM A COMPLETELY FULFILLED WOMAN. A fulfilled woman is one whose desires to give and receive Love is fully realized. This affirmation alone can change your life completely. The way to happiness is discovering and fulfilling your true desires.

Print this affirmation and place where you will see it several times a day – We know that you will find amazing results.

Stay in your feeling nature as much as possible, as you say these affirmations. When finished, call them Good. You may experience heightened desires, and expand your acceptance of Love. These are greater expressions of your feeling nature. If you have repressed your sexuality, these new or increased feelings may also create fear, or self-judgment. Pray about it. Life is now, and we live it by prayer.

Please add these affirmations to your list and enjoy them daily.

> I have all that Universal Woman has.
> I have an infinite amount of Woman Love to express.
> I praise and love my womb, the secret and hallowed place of creation, the most precious place in every woman's body. It is the treasure of the human race.

I bless the beautiful channel to my womb. It is a warm and tender and flowing with love.

I praise the glorious flower of my clitoris, whose only function is to give pleasure to me and my partner.

I love and praise my breasts, belly, my back and buttocks - every part of my ecstatic feminine body.

My physical being expresses, receives and communicates Spiritual Love.

Notes

LESSON SEVEN

The Partner You Desire

"The perfect man [or partner] will appear, when the perfect woman [or partner] is there to claim him."[or her]."

EMMET FOX, NEW THOUGHT LEADER AND FOUNDER OF DIVINE SCIENCE

THIS CHAPTER IS to clarify your desires about having a partner. Some women feel complete without a partner and some women feel incomplete without a partner. Let us take a look at where we stand on the subject and why. Get a journal or paper and pen ready; you are about to take a quiz. Take as much time as you need, and write a brief, clearly stated answer to the following questions.

1. Is there currently a partner in your life? (husband, wife, lover, life partner)
2. If so, what pleases you the most about your partner?
3. If not a partner, why not? What decisions or choices have you made that stop you from having a partner?
4. If not in the present, was there a partner at another time?
5. What is your honest opinion of the most important partner in your life (past or present) In addition to your opinion, list this person's strengths and best qualities.
6. Now make a separate list of this person's weaknesses, or faults.
7. What qualities do you desire to add to your current partnership, or wish to experience in a future partnership?

Do not be afraid of being totally honest. If you are holding negative opinions about any partner, past or present, this is a good time to face them. After one clear look at any negativity, we shall set about to create a healing experience.

As to the first question, there is a male in every woman's life, in the present or past. A father, brother, husband, (or ex-husband) priest or pastor, have all contributed to our opinions about men. If you are not presently enjoying a loving relationship with a man or men in general, let this be as a conscious choice, rather than of rejection from hurtful experiences or negative judgments that need to be healed. Painful memories, left without healing can stop you for life. This lesson may help you with a beautiful healing.

Women today are more independent than ever and many openly state they have no need for a man. If you are a heterosexual woman who has declared that statement and suddenly an Angel of God stood before you and introduced you to "The Perfect Man", how would you react? Would you say "No thanks" or "Thank you, God"?

It is still your choice. Stay with this lesson, heal what is needed, then ask yourself the same question. If your response is different write to us, as we would love to hear about it.

Let us define and emphasize the point of needing a partner or desiring a partner. Need is a condition, as if you are somehow incomplete without a partner. Desire is the foundation of creativity. Desiring a partner, drives one to create a relationship, hopefully, and for our purposes, based on Love.

If the idea of a man in your life is interwoven with ideas of fear, guilt, or some sort of bondage or painful memories, we ask, *have you at any time ever known some wonderful man?* If you have, then know that his qualities are true qualities that exist within every man in the world, for underneath every false appearance, is a beautiful soul.

Many prayer teams receive prayer requests for the "perfect partner". The truth is, we draw unto ourselves according to our beliefs and opinions. If our opinion of a potential partner is that they are insensitive or selfish, we will continue those qualities in a partner, over and over again. Got guilt? You get brutality. Got a lack of confidence? You get the controlling, domineering type. Feeling motherly? You get the weakling, or childish partner to mother or manage. Get the picture? So who needs to adjust their beliefs?

In Truth, everyone has within them, as they were created – Perfection in Spirit. Everyone was created by a Perfect God. However as much perfection as we have within, we are still living within our basic natures, all human qualities, from the lowest to the highest. We are also living in the composite mind of the human race which contains much error beliefs. What we experience in life depends on which beliefs we identify with, what we are willing to tune in to. Just like hundreds of choices on cable TV, we choose that with which we are most comfortable. If you decide a particular channel is not for your best interest, you may change it, and its influence can be erased. However, if you get careless, or re-engage with the same old thoughts, an old issue can reappear. It only means that you tuned into it. You can once again - tune it out.

Your partner may be one way in the world and completely different with you. Whichever aspect of them you tune into, that is what you will experience. It is all about what you believe – really believe – about them. As we know, our consciousness is comprised of both our conscious and sub-conscious minds. Whatever your beliefs are, it will be reflected in your relationship. Look again at your "Fault list" – this is a reflection of your beliefs that must be healed in order to transform your experience.

If you do not have a partner, or think you don't even want one, it is possible that your beliefs are so ingrained in fearful thought patterns, that no potential partner dares to come into your life. Are your thoughts about this based on your past? Do not despair, for a belief is only an idea held in mind and it can be replaced with a new, opposite idea that will result in a completely different experience.

This concept works in all relationships, but our focus is on Loving Partner relationships.

Many women long for a better relationship in their present partnership. When we meet difficult problems in a relationship, sometimes we think the solution is leaving the relationship completely or to withdraw mentally. Sometimes we think that another partner is what we need. The *Grass is Greener* effect is an illusion. For guess what goes with you when you leave – your emotional baggage – which includes all your beliefs about your partner and yourself. So there is still much work to be done.

This is not an anti-divorce statement, this is a *Get-Real-And-Work-On-Yourself* statement, with or without your partner. Sometimes a relationship can take you down some dark roads. It is important to keep your spiritual values intact and know that you can create a life you love, with or without a partner.

If you leave a relationship, it is most important to heal the relationship through forgiveness, contemplation and a healing of your old beliefs. After all, you do not want to re-create the exact same relationship problems again. Often when this happens, the problems actually accelerate to an even more painful experience. Leave if you must; work on your healing belief systems; recreate a new healthy, happy life.

God can work in any place, and in any relationship. No more self-delusion; you are free to choose the life you were born to live. It is important for both you and any partner to understand each other's life purpose, to respect each other's path and to work out a way to keep those paths compatible.

If we can sustain a consciousness of Oneness in Universal Love, loving each other will be natural. Imagine what a wonderful world that would be. We all desire Love, and if we can become instruments of God's Love, we can heal each other. Let's go with God, work on ourselves in this lesson and make our own little corner of the world a place where Love flows beautifully.

Before we begin the Steps to Healing… we want to look at any resistance that may be welling up inside you. That is a clear signal that you would benefit from this process. Many women want to skip this process and move on to the next chapter. We ask you to embrace this healing process and realize that you will see yourself and past relationships with new eyes. You can release the past in this gentle process.

STEP ONE: THE HEALING OF PAST RELATIONSHIPS

If there is a lack of Love in your life, find the truth about your opinion of the men in your life. Is there some memory of hurt, failure, or guilt in the depths of your mind? Is there some recurring pattern in your experience in connection with a man?

The following exercise has helped many women gain happier relationships with her partner. For this exercise, please arrange for three or four hours, when you may be alone and uninterrupted. Have a journal or paper and pen ready.

Begin by going back to your earliest memories of the first man in your life. For most women, this would be your father. Take as much time as you need and write down as many memories as you have of this person. Review them one by one, and write next to each one – How you honestly felt at each of these experiences. Then talk to him as if he were in the room with you.

Linda's Example: "Dad, I remember when you would take us for a Sunday drive and we would stop for ice cream. That was fun and I loved that we our family had Sunday afternoons together."

"Dad, I remember when you used to help me with my math homework. You would get so angry with me if I didn't get it right. I felt like I was not very smart and that I disappointed you."

"Dad, I remember when you taught me to ice skate. I loved it! I also remember when you tried to teach me to dive into a swimming pool. I couldn't do it correctly and you quit trying and I quit trying. I felt like there was something wrong with me."

Can you begin to see the seeds of Linda's feelings toward men? She developed self-doubt, and worthiness issues. Thinking that there is something wrong with you will deplete you self-worth and affect *all* your choices in life.

Now, you begin the forgiveness process. Take each instance again, for example:

"Dad, I completely forgive you for all the times we argued over math homework. I know you were doing the best you could to help me understand it. I know you wanted me to excel in math for good reasons."

Then speak to that same child that still lives within you…

"_____ (use your name/nickname) I see that you were very frustrated and hurt by your father's exasperation at trying to help you with your math homework. He wanted you to be brilliant, and what you didn't realize is that you are brilliant. I see you as an analytical genius. You made it with great grades, yes with his help, but with your own abilities. I love you." Wrap your arms around that child, tell her you are pleased with her and will always be there for her. Give her the nurturing she may have missed as a child.

Then forgive yourself, the adult, who has carried these feelings for a lifetime. Proclaim that the past has been released forever, and no longer has any power in your life. Claim your newness as a woman, now capable of greater expressions of Love.

Repeat this process for as long as it takes you to feel ready to go on to the next step.

Note: I have done this work as part of a life-changing weekend intensive workshop. It was an incredibly liberating experience, and for some a gut-wrenching experience, yet nonetheless liberating.

STEP TWO: THE HEALING OF PRESENT RELATIONSHIPS

Most women are always ready to make improvements in their current relationships. Have pen and paper or your journal ready and again, take as much time as you need.

Go back to your original list of your partner's faults. Now write a corresponding list, writing down the opposite trait for each of the faults.

Example: #1. My partner is not affectionate and ignores me.

Now write: #1. My partner is warm, affectionate and genuinely interested in my happiness. (Even if this appears to you as an absolute lie – write it down anyway.)

Go through the entire list, writing down the new statements.

Now shred, or burn or tear up the old fault list. Let the Light of Truth beam from your heart to your partner's heart.

Read the new statements aloud, and declare them as your new truth. Say it like you mean it and believe it. The new beliefs have now been established in your mind, and the results will increasingly become your true experience.

Step Three: Daily Affirmations of the Truth
Next, you will begin the daily work of affirming My Perfect Partner. As you are repeating your affirmations with the Universal Woman Treatment, you are to add the My Perfect Partner to your daily work. Be ready to have the right person appear.

Remember that you are not trying to manipulate or change anyone. You are accepting that the best of you is coming forward to meet the best in your existing or potential partner. None of us is equipped with enough understanding to know what could be changed in another person. We are simply affirming the best truths of ourselves and affirming our awareness of the best in another person.

Several times throughout this course, we have discussed the detriment of judgment. Now we are working on the acceptance of the truth, which creates the opportunity for the very best in someone to shine. This is how we create future relationships. We state the Truth, and that which is less than the Truth, will fall away.

Now, carefully read the next section titled Accepting the Perfect Partner, (aloud if possible) and reinforce each word with all the belief you can express. Most of this treatment is self-explanatory. You can expect an awakening, and you will receive the benefits of a rekindling of your partner's interests and desires. You partner does not even need to know what it is you are doing. Your mental vibrations are changing and it is natural for your partner to respond.

If you have a desire for more love in your life, remember that nature is on your side; life is on your side; God is on your side, for God *is* Love! Be diligent about your mental work, and the results will follow.

Please put the name of your existing partner in the blank line.

If you are seeking to see the truth of a relationship with a particular person, then put that name in the blank space.

You may also simply use the words My Partner.

Accepting the Perfect Partner

My Perfect Partner:
_____ is Life, God, expressing as a whole, complete person.
_____ is a Complete Masculine-Feminine Being expressing as a _____.
_____ is created by God, and is honest, perfect and true.
_____ is a unique, natural, individual expression of all_____.

My Perfect Partner:
_____ is all that _____ is created to be.
_____ is beauty, love, warmth, vigor, strength, power perfect form, assertive, giving, direct, fearless, daring, resilient, joy and wisdom.
_____ has a great sense of humor and is a joy to be with.
_____ is gorgeous, all confident, magnetic and undeniable.

My Perfect Partner
_____ has Universal, ever-present, free, pure, all-intense desire for me.
_____ has a powerful drive to pursue me.
_____ completely accepts me and us as perfect partners.
_____ and I fulfill each other's desires.

My Perfect Partner
_____ knows that we are perfect for each other, spiritually, mentally, and physically.
_____ knows all there is to know about sex and is completely confident in expressing it with me.
_____ is completely in love with me.
_____ is free from any judgment or rejection of me.
_____ has no barriers between us.
_____ accepts me as a perfect mate.
_____ takes a rightful side by side relationship with me.
_____ is self-loving, life-loving and together we express all that we are and all we are meant to be.

My PERFECT MARRIAGE

I thank God, for my perfect marriage. I thank God that the masculine and feminine in me are balanced in a perfect state of understanding, acceptance, love, joy, fascination, excitement, and ecstasy. This is the truth of my natures as I am a complete, integrated being, a Person of God.

All I desire in a partner, is within me. Nothing can take this away from me. The Unity of my own male/female natures within, creates for my outer life a beautiful expression of unity and love.

I Am In Love

I am in love with the perfect partner, and my partner is wholly and completely in love with me. I am complete fulfillment, heaven for my partner, as my partner is for me. I am infinitely valuable to my partner, as my partner is to me. We greatly desire each other. My partner loves to pursue me and I love to be pursued by my partner.

There is absolutely no separation, lack, or rejection between my partner and me. There is only acceptance and joy. There is no fear between my partner and me. We are one in God.

I am free and fulfilled, in all ways.

I am a perfect woman in a perfect love affair, with my perfect partner. We share perfect understanding, communication, expression and fulfillment in Universal Love. Thank you, God!

Before we move on to Lesson Eight...

There are many circumstances that may have formulated your opinions of yourself and experiences which have affected your consciousness in ways in which you are not fully aware. All of us have endured painful situations that continue to influence or manipulate our actions and define our self-worth. This is the emotional baggage previously referred to on page 55. We all have it. The past is just energy and we all must release it.

As women move forward to create new pathways for equality and peace, we must release the resentments held over the centuries of oppression of women. We must look at this with a viewpoint of an ever evolving Spirit within. We must forgive ourselves for fearfully accepting concepts of weakness, or worthlessness.

We have paid a dear price and some women still are paying for the price of fear. It is a form of bondage. Emancipate yourself from fears. Clean out that place where you've stored that baggage, pack it and don't give it to anyone else. Don't bury it; that's called denial. Create a ceremony and burn it. Liberate yourself and do it with deep sincere prayer. We can release the victim, forever.

This is a great subject for women's healing circles. Until I first came to this chapter, I did not realize how much my interactions with my father had created a pattern of choices that continued through my adult life. Sometimes we need one on one therapy to recognize these patterns and ways to create new, healthier choices. Stay with Spirit and you'll be led to the right teachers.

The Identity Intensive, mentioned earlier was a powerful weekend experience that changed my life. It was designed by Robert Lorenz, PhD. We spent several hours looking at the characteristics of one parent and identifying which of these characteristics we had adapted and those we rejected. We repeated the same process with the other parent. [There is much more to this than can be put in a paragraph.] In the end my greatest discoveries were that the things I liked the most about myself were characteristics that did not relate to either parent. I discovered my own true identity, and as Shakespeare said, "To thine own self be true".

All of humankind is evolving and for us to look forward with high expectations we can no longer dwell in the energies of the past. Let God declare amnesty for the oppressors when we can't.

Surrender that which no longer serves us, then proclaim and accept your greatest freedom. Let us move onward.

LESSON EIGHT

Acceptance of the Body
Natural Poise – Grace – Lasting Youth

"Taking care of the body is an act of Grace. Embrace the body with Love and it will become the willing servant to the goals of Spirit."

PAUL FERRINI, AUTHOR, SPIRITUAL LEADER

ACCEPTANCE IS THE strong magnet which attracts more value to your life. It is the realization of the truth about you as a woman, which can be life-changing. Acceptance is not just acknowledgement or tolerance. Real acceptance is wholehearted. True acceptance of the body includes healthy, unabashed sensuality and moves all the way to enjoyment. It is the savoring of all the body pleasures.

Toddlers naturally take great pleasure in their bodies and all of their bodily functions. This freedom is soon diminished as standards of propriety and correctness are taught. Children today are little athletes by the time they enter kindergarten, running back and forth across soccer fields all over the country. Fitness regimes are part of the American lifestyle for teenagers and adults. Yet, the United States has a huge problem with obesity in both children and adults. Is all the blame to be placed on the American diet? Or is it more? Is it our sense of worth? Can we look at our bodies as a beautiful Divine gift and teach this to our children, while accepting this truth for ourselves?

For the purposes of this book, let us look at our own body. It is a Divine gift of great value and a treasure of pleasure. Even breathing can be considered a pleasure when done consciously. Taking in long, deep, slow breaths of fresh air brings both peace and a smile. A morning stretch is a great pleasure from head to toe. Why? Because it is focused appreciation. Yoga practices can also be considered focused appreciation of the body. Have you ever heard a woman say, "I hate my Yoga classes"? No, not ever. We usually hear women say, "I wish I could take more classes, I love how I feel when my body is completely stretched out and I gain more flexibility." These classes are always done in a peaceful environment.

Anytime you dance, your body brings you pleasure. Dance is good for the brain, good for the body; good for the soul. Enjoy your body! Dance is done in a stimulating environment and creates laughter and fun.

Making love to your partner is meant to bring great pleasure to both of you. The environment may be peaceful or stimulating, for neither matters. It is the focused appreciation of Loving bodies, which heightens the desires and the experience.

All of the above body exercises require your self-acceptance. You do not have to have the body of a teenaged cheerleader to move in a way that gives you healthy pleasures. The key to uninhibited pleasure is self-acceptance. When you come to the state of loving and accepting your body as a beautiful gift, your self-respect, self-confidence, and self-love will enhance all areas of your life. Your creativity will escalate, your relationships improve, and your sensuality will intensify.

Once upon a time, a nod and a handshake was the accepted greeting for our society. Men always extended a hand. Women kept their gloves on, lightly touched hands, and smiled. Now the gloves are off, and men, women and children willingly hug each other as a loving greeting. Freely expressing physical tenderness relaxes people and lifts the human spirit. Thank you God, for that step in the evolution of the human spirit.

If you belong to a church or other spiritual community, it is natural to see people greet each other by hugging one another. If there is a "greet your neighbor" segment in your Sunday service, you may see total strangers embrace. It is a pleasure to exchange or share positive body vibrations with one another in this simple manner. (On three separate occasions recently, congregants have told me they come to church for the hugs!)

For a greater acceptance of your body, you must increase your love toward your body. Think about what you put into it and on it. Begin with the acceptance of *"This body is a gift from God"*. Know that the essence of you is not your body, but that learning to love and cherish your body will transform your expressions of health and vitality. Be good to yourself. Start accepting the Love.

Several years ago, my *California Girl* daughter took residence in Montreal, Canada for a year. While there, she was in a loving relationship with a young man who came from a wonderful, large Italian family. During a holiday weekend, all the family gathered at a beautiful lake and had a delightful time. They were picnicking, swimming, and laughing and enjoying themselves. The following Monday, my daughter called to share her insights about this event. She said, "Mom, it was fabulous, all ages had a great time. All sizes wore bathing suits and enjoyed swimming in the lake. Nobody cared who was a plus size or what kind of bathing suit they were wearing. They were who they were and just enjoyed each other."

In the USA, we are bombarded with innumerable diets, fashion mandates and a false culture of beauty. This "Accepting and Loving my body" may sound difficult, even akin to mountain climbing. The truth is, it is not about thinking, "Well, I guess I have to make do with what I've got." Want to transform what you've got? Start loving it, finding value in every part of your body, will make you feel alive. You will find changes you hadn't even considered. Begin with gratitude for the body the Love of God has given you. Use the affirmations at the end of this lesson and observe the changes that will happen right before your eyes.

Dignity, once meant to behave with formality and pride in oneself. Dignity today, means to retain your self-respect, worthiness, and standards. It is not about what society demands of you, but about being true to yourself.

A female potter in the process of creating beautiful pottery, splattered with mud while at the wheel, is a dignified artist. If that same woman attended a dinner party still splattered with the mud, she may not appear to be as dignified.

<u>True dignity is honesty of expression in tune with the situation at hand and showing self-respect and respect for others.</u>

Renowned Orchestral Conductor, Arthur Fiedler, conducted the Boston Pops Orchestra for fifty years. (1930-1980) At the finale of the Boston Pops concerts he would delight his audiences with a medley of current popular music, expertly arranged, and played with pure joy. Once at a concert in San Diego, he arrived on the scene on a fire engine with sirens sounding and lights flashing, receiving a standing ovation before the concert even began. Fiedler had a lifetime expression of his pure Love for music. This is an example of exuberant enthusiasm about life. Don't we all want to feel like this on our life's path?

Today, we see a "push the envelope" culture in the entertainment industry, and throughout society. Often, this creates a huge amount of attention, media blitz, sold-out concerts, films, etc. and great fortunes. On the other side of this entertainment coin, we read of alcohol and drug addictions and suicides. What is missing here is a sense of balance and a sense of spirituality to guide one on a healthy path of free expression. The Love factor is missing. When pure Love of artistic expression is prevalent there is joy and enthusiasm for life.

Another area for women to perhaps see differently is "The Madison Avenue Effect". Since the 1920's, the advertising industry has manipulated the American public into believing that beauty, love, attractiveness, wealth, health, etc., all come from some product someone is trying to sell. An example of that process for women is over time we have moved from corsets to girdles to push-up bras and tight body-shapers. Did you know that the tradition of a diamond engagement ring came from an advertising campaign in the early 20th century titled "A Diamond is Forever"? Does the car you drive actually make you sexy or alluring? These are powerful images we are bombarded with daily. Let's choose differently. Being true to yourself creates clarity of personal choice and greater self-respect rather than egoist, prideful illusions.

The Divine Feminine, the Universal Woman knows exactly who she is, and how to freely express herself.

As a woman learns to love, honor and praise her own body, she makes choices that enhance her inner strength, physical and emotional health, and the development of body wisdom, through her awareness of Spirit within.

The Truth is that the Life Force of God, lives within every cell of your body, and through the recognition of this Truth we can maintain our health, and freely express all that we are and all we are meant to be.

Poise and Grace, are synonymous and defined as a sense of freedom and confidence; to be in command of the situation at hand through self-assurance, self-confidence, which is achieved through self-awareness. Knowing who you really are produces balance, dignity, poise and pure thinking. You are the feminine aspect of Spirit.

Self-doubt or rejection robs us of our potential. So let us remain constant with our prayers to dissolve any false beliefs about ourselves. Let us be compelled to do the best we can at all times. Do not hinder your future by holding on to the past. Conquer and release any old feelings of guilt, and forgive yourself for your past mistakes. Releasing the past allows the Grace of God to unfold before you.

Every day brings you a new, clean slate to recreate your life. God gives us each day to fill it with positive possibilities, golden opportunities, and greater expressions of Love. Look to who you really are, rather than who you once were, or even who you were yesterday.

Rev. Ann Meyer stated: *"I really believe there is no such thing as failure. We either have a success or a learning experience – never a failure. Failure is only the beginning of a new learning experience; success is the ending of an old one."*

<u>The secret of poise is the ceasing of all criticism</u> – of the self and of others. This is the challenge of self-acceptance. Self-criticism is the enemy. Silence that false inner voice that tells you what you are not and affirm the truth of who you are. When this becomes your manner, you will find yourself walking, speaking, acting, and expressing with perfect natural poise, personal style and grace.

Lasting Youth – Rev. Ann Meyer once wrote, *"When I was young in age, I was quite old in spirit, as was reflected in the tediousness of my living, [reflected by] the serious look on my face and the rigid restrictions of my life expression. I am discovering more and more each year of how to enjoy life; how to be free, enthusiastic and happy. Youth is not a matter of years, but of attitude."*

Youth is spontaneity - Youth is honesty. Stay in the present moment and respond freshly and creatively to situations. How many times have you heard the comment *"Well, the way we always did it before was…?"* This is old habit, half-dormant thinking and dulls our life experience. We can all benefit by removing layer upon layer of dull thinking revealing our inner brilliance by staying present and getting off of the auto-pilot mode. Life changes quickly and the young are excited about it and the old resist it. Which would you rather be known for?

For this week's lesson, try to observe your responses to your daily life. When you open your eyes in the morning are you grateful for another day? Do you have the same greeting for your loved ones? When someone asks you how you are today – do you habitually answer, "I'm fine". Break that habit!

Charles Fillmore, Unity co-founder, wrote in his 94th year: *"I fairly sizzle with zeal and enthusiasm and spring forth with a mighty faith to do the things that ought to be done by me!"* How often are your responses to your work, your family or friends, filled with such vitality? Create your own sense of enthusiasm using your own words. Write them down and say them often.

Find meaning and purpose in all that you do this week. Look for the beauty in your day. Don't give a reciprocal kiss to your partner – give an enthusiastic – *I love life and I love you* - kind of kiss. Keep the passion in your life.

Don't let your sexual expressions fall into habitual predictability. This happens easily in a marriage, AND you can recreate the passion, freshness and spontaneity. It is never too late, as long as there is love.

Youth is Flexibility. Youth looks at change as a field of possibilities. Flexibility is the key to being present to the Presence of God. It is a release of fear and resistance that allows change to help you grow and stay young.

I would like to share a story of a woman who came to our church, bubbling over with enthusiasm. She smiled the biggest smile her face could make. This is her story….she is a Certified Life Coach, which means that she has had training to help you discover what your talents and abilities are and support you in the fulfillment of your dreams. She already had the skills to identify that which she had within herself to recreate her life. She and her husband (now deceased) had always had horses, and her new dream was to combine her love of horses and to work as a coach in a camp for children with special needs. She began her search for such a center and found that in order to move forward, she needed extra training and certification to do this kind work. After an extensive search to locate a place to attain this certification, she applied.

She came to my office one day in a state of bliss, to share that she had been accepted for the perfect program and was well on her way to the fulfillment of her dream. There would be many changes yet to come, but she was more than willing. The best part of this story is that in a few weeks our friend was about to celebrate her 75th birthday. She was as exuberant as a teenager who just got accepted at the college of her dreams. In fact, that is how she said she felt. Now that is lasting youth.

Life is change, whether we like it or not. Sometimes changes come unexpectedly and we want to fold our tent, draw the shades, and stay under the covers. The truth is that no matter how hard it is to see it, the Goodness of God is always constant; the form it shows up in may be temporary. As we realize this, we find that within the peace of God there is no fear; we are comforted and can trust that the next good thing in life is out there in front of us. Welcome and embrace change, for it will bring you lasting youth.

Youth is being in Love. Showing enthusiasm for Life brings Love to all that you do. Love your job, your home, your wardrobe, your car, as they are all gifts. Take care of them to the best of your ability. My friend Mona used to eat every meal like it was the best meal she ever ate. She used to say it out loud, with enthusiasm, *"Those were the best eggs and pancakes I ever ate!"* I would often respond with *"You said that yesterday."* What I hadn't realized, was the love and enthusiasm with which she ate had an amazing effect on her metabolism. She was slim and trim, while if I looked at pancakes for breakfast, I was sure I would put on two more pounds by lunch. Get the picture? The more Love you put into your daily expressions of life – the more Goodness of God – the best of everything comes your way.

Be in love, feel the love, put more love in your relationships, your work, your home and your spiritual life. Be Love in Action. All this love will have an anti-aging effect on your mind and body.

Please add these affirmations to your list………..

Explanations of Affirmations for Acceptance - Lesson Eight

I embrace acceptance of my own body. I love and accept my body as a gift from God. I am grateful for all my physical attributes and senses. I release all old ideas, and criticisms about my body, right now, in this very moment. My gratitude for this body enhances all the best of me and as I appreciate my body. It improves in new and exciting ways.

I humbly, and lovingly accept myself and the Goodness of God in my daily life. I can love myself by knowing that I am a Woman of God. I myself, do nothing, as it is the Grace of the Presence within that does it all. All that I am, all my good, is a demonstration of God's love for me.

I create new levels of Joy in my life. As I consciously create new and greater expressions of love and gratitude for my talents and abilities, Joy appears in new, unexpected and exciting ways.

I have the sparkle of youth. I live my life motivated by love and bring enthusiasm to all that I do. It is contagious and I see it reflecting in my family, friends and co-workers.

I am a free, natural woman and am an instrument of God's Love. From head to toe, I feel alive, awake and enthusiastic. I am created with God-given purpose, talents, and abilities and successfully express them as God intended, and therefore cannot be denied. I Trust God, wholly and completely.

Affirmations - Lesson Eight

I embrace acceptance of my own body.

I humbly and lovingly accept myself and the Goodness of God in my life.

I create new levels of Joy in my life.

I have the sparkle of youth.

I am a free, natural woman and am an instrument of God's Love.

Notes

LESSON NINE

Love's Expression of Freedom

"To know yourself as the Being underneath the thinker, the stillness underneath the mental noise, the love and joy underneath the pain, is freedom, salvation, enlightenment."

ECKHART TOLLE

FREEDOM IS A most basic and necessary factor of love. Without freedom, there can be no real love. Love is a strong and hardy thing. In fact, real love is invincible and can overcome all obstacles placed before it. Love is also fragile in a certain way. If love is denied its freedom – it disappears, leaving something else in its place – something that resembles love, but is not love. It may be called loyalty, resolution, duty, dependency, insecurity, or pretense. Whatever it is…it is not love.

Love must be free like a beautiful, shining bubble floating freely and changing as it reflects the life about it. Yet if someone tries to catch and hold on to it, it is gone. Love must be free not to love before it can be free to love. The idea of possession is not compatible with the idea of love. When freedom is denied by thoughts or actions, neither the possessor nor the possessed is able to feel love.

Let us create a story, titled **"The Path of Possessive Love".** You get to be the lead character in this story, so be a star and let yourself feel all the feelings of the lover's journey.

Our story opens at the path where love begins. You find yourself in the place where potential lovers are first aware of an attraction for one another. This first scene is that wonderful place where you may feel physically attracted to someone. You pick the scenery. The feeling is kind of exciting – Right? You are not being urged, coerced or told that it is your duty to fall in love. No one is telling you that it is your moral duty to be attracted to this person. This happens to you with complete freedom, thus the attraction is natural and thrilling. At this point both of you are completely free. No one has to account to the other. No one is responsible for the other. Each is attracted to the other exactly as they see them. This **"Attraction Stage"** is a building stage for real love.

Next, you have lighthearted conversations with this person which moves toward the possibility of the two of you getting to know each other. If the attraction grows increasingly stronger, you effortlessly move into the **"Magnetism Stage"**. This can be blissful and filled with the promise of joy. Whatever is going on in the world seems inconsequential. Each of you are on your best behavior and of course, hiding your worst behaviors. Each, looks perfect to the other and this is fabulous.

Now you are moving into the **"Acceptance Stage"**. At this point, even your lover's faults appear as a virtues. For example: that miserly behavior appears as wisely frugal; and that stubborn streak appears as steadfast determination. You are in a place of non-judgment. You praise each other for these wonderful virtues. At last, you have found the love you have been searching for. This is actually a place of wisdom. At this point, some would say you are in the *Love is Blind* mode, but actually you are seeing with the *Eyes of Love*. It's true – maybe heart to heart – soul to soul, but not the whole truth.

In the natural course of events, you develop the **"Tenderness and Understanding Stage"**. You each begin to reveal your *story* of life experiences. You share your childhood and past experiences that you find meaningful, carefully leaving out details you prefer not to share. Your potential partner does the same. You look at each other's strengths and weaknesses as even more reasons to love this person. Weaknesses? All this person needs is a good woman like you to fix everything – Right?

Then, you find an even more intense desire to be together. There is *Excitement* in a phone call, *Creative Expression* in planning your next date, and you are moving quickly into the **"Passion Stage"**. What an intoxicating feeling! Notice as you play this part, how much energy you have. You want this person by your side and you think about them from the time you get up in the morning until you go to sleep at night. Nothing else seems more important. You have to be together. Your heart is full and you feel that together you can achieve anything.

As your story progresses, you now find that you are ready for the highest peak of Love - The **"Union Stage"**. You move in together or are now planning a marriage. It's your story – so you decide… You may plan a fabulous wedding, or a romantic elopement, the decision is to be united forever. This is *the One* - Glory be to God – We're in Heaven!

Intermission – also known as the Honeymoon

You now have **"The License"**. You have made a commitment to each other. A legal and binding commitment. The two of you are now one and you realize that there are rules of engagement – Right? Somehow, the idea of ownership has seeped into the picture. We call it *belonging* to each other. *I am yours – you are mine, and that is good.* The truth is…you are a tad confused.

Now our story takes on a bit of a change. You are looking at your proprietary rights and expectations. You are tired, you work hard and just don't feel the need to put forward your best every day. You naturally relax into those patterns or habits you so skillfully managed to control in the "Tenderness and Understanding Stage". You start thinking…*Why don't they understand and just cooperate?* This is the **"Path of Possessive Love"** and it is a slippery downward slope that appears much too quickly. It is based on false ideas and leads to confusion in the minds of both of you. Can you feel the confusion?

When you own something, you are responsible for it – Right? Now, suddenly, there is trouble. *By the way…where did all that energy go?* You are trying hard to understand what has happened. You think to yourself…*we are partners, I feel responsible for my partner, and they represent my choice.* Now you are concerned about everything they do….including how they are wearing their hair. Hmmm…could that be the ego?

The truth is - No human being was ever meant to own or be owned by another human being. You are not to possess or be possessed. Not your body – Not your mind.

In truth, you are perfect, and you are free.

Love is about the wisdom of the heart.

Now back to our story………….

Time marches on and you are having friends over for dinner one night, and you notice that your partner seems to be attracted to your best friend. You do your best not to, but you feel wildly jealous and terribly guilty for even suspecting such a thing. So you repress those feelings deep inside, because it just couldn't be so! You *belong* to each other. So where do you think those feelings went? Now as time goes on, each time your best friend wants to visit, you make excuses and a plan to visit her separately from your spouse. Seems like a fair compromise - Right? Actually, it brings up the original jealousy and guilt, all over again. Now you have to "own" those feelings in a degree equal to the degree of possessiveness you have created, through your false ideas.

Then, as your false ideas continue…

You are planning a future together, so you have expectations. We all have desires, dreams and expectations for results. The problem comes when your communications begin to sound like demands. Demands that come from your self-righteousness as a good partner. Unfortunately, your partner already thinks you are a good partners and is offended by your demands. You still love this person, but you think you have now discovered that your partner is not perfect. Instead of denying your desires, or forcing an issue, you begin to close your heart. You are obviously, incredibly disappointed.

Then one Sunday you go to church and you find out that if you followed Spiritual Law, you can and must make all your demands upon God, where all things are possible. Demanding anything from your partner is not ever going to work. Demanding that the Universe supply all your needs and fulfill all your desires creates infinite possibilities. You now have a new way of looking at your life and your marriage. Now there is the possibility of miracles. You have hope.

Like everyone else on the planet, you have listened to the voice of the inner-critic for almost your entire life. Somehow, that voice is not just criticizing you, now it is also criticizing your partner. When you were first falling in love, you barely heard this voice. Now you're keenly aware of your partner's faults. Have they changed? What you haven't realized is, in the oneness of your union, each time you have criticized your mate, you have criticized yourself. Have you noticed that this is not doing wonders for your sex life? Okay, you can have good sex or criticism – Which would you like?

As time moves forward we have to take a good, hard look at this union and evaluate it and your future together. Now you have to make some decisions. I mean after all, you had this big wedding, (*we knew you would make that choice*) you are buying a house, and you really do want to have children. You can make this work. So you have to overlook a few things, so what. *It's not like I don't feel any love. Everybody does it – Right? We promised love, honor and loyalty. So I will always be respectful, and stay loyal.*

What happens when that loyalty trickles down into your kisses, your love-making, and confuses the purity and power of attraction and desire? Are you enjoying passionate hellos and goodbyes? Do you look at your partner with tenderness and a deep yearning for each other as you did in the "**Magnetism Stage**"?

You can only go downhill from here or you can live a depressing, dutiful charade.

Now What?

Remember that Sunday you went to a Spiritual Center and were told that you could make demands on the Universe instead of your partner? As long as there is honesty and love, you can recreate your relationship. It's time for prayer. It's time to re-open your heart and see your partner with compassion. It is time to turn within and reconnect with your **Spiritual Freedom** and work these principles into your daily life. **You can reconnect with your own Inner Self and find the wisdom and power you need to return to real love.**

Start with daily meditation, even if it is only ten minutes each morning, you will find the presence of the Universal Woman within. Listen to her, she will guide you, nurture you, and you will feel her love. You will be led to right ideas, right activities, improved relationships, and greater freedom to grow and become more of who you are really meant to be.

Next, it is time to let go of old restrictive beliefs and gain **Mental Freedom.** It is time to let go of the past, destructive habits, and fear-based decisions that created that slippery downward slope of your self-worth and the rejection of your partner. It is time to allow a new relationship to emerge. A new relationship with yourself first. It is time for a return to Love.

Try this affirming thought…**From now on**…"**I resolve to be true to myself, my Highest Self, The Supreme Being, which is God. The Law of God sets me free, to be made new. My highest and best good is at hand. Right here – Right now."**

This is God's First Commandment – "Thou shalt place no other God's before me."

As you accept this freedom, you give others that same freedom. Which means, you now release all judgment and criticism, and move forward into **Acceptance** through eyes of Love.

Then there is **Forgiveness** – daily prayers for forgiveness of yourself and your beloved. No one has the perfect marriage or partnership, all the time. We all slip into humanness now and then, yet you want to live in harmony. To do that you must examine your mind and heart, to free yourself. The question is "Am I living in fear or faith?" Your faith must be based in Love.

Emotional Freedom comes when you have forgiven and released the past and fully accepted who you are and what you desire for yourself. Release the *woulda-coulda-shoulda* dialogue, accepting all that you are so that you can truly see the person with whom you are trying to be true. Become the heart centered compassionate woman who is tender with herself. Then, do the same with your partner. In this, you will find gratitude, which is the pathway to happiness and freedom.

Can you see how this **"Path of Possessive Love"** can both create and destroy a relationship? It is easy to use the old adage "To each his own" when you are speaking about an acquaintance, but in a committed relationship – it's a challenge. Yet, through this challenge you can create a bond, rather than bondage. You can keep your love fresh, and exciting rather than habitual or boring. You can create a dynamic future, rather than live by obligatory responsibilities. How can you be depressed in a relationship that is mentally, physically, emotionally and spiritually thriving?

Back to our story….

How does this story end? It is your story and you have the freedom to decide.

Love always has the answer. You have the tools to recreate your path to loving relationships through **Love's Freedom of Expression**. It cannot be determined by the world outside of you, but by the beautiful, peace filled, world within you. You can meet any challenge with the wisdom of the heart. Where there is peace, there is no fear. Where there is forgiveness, there is growth and expansion. Where there is gratitude, there is joy.

Notes

LESSON TEN

The Love Meditation

IF YOU HAVE been diligent with your affirmations and meditations during the past nine weeks, you have no doubt stirred new feelings within yourself and noticed positive changes in several areas of your life, particularly in your relationships. The culmination of this course is The Love Meditation. You will find it at the end of the Affirmation and Meditation section of the book.

The Universal Woman is the feeling nature of humankind. The acceptance and realization of this Divine Feminine Nature will bring the power of Love into all that you do, for it is how we feel that creates our beliefs and our beliefs manifest in how we see ourselves and how we live.

Every individual has a different concept of what Love really is. Perhaps like God, we may never fully comprehend or define exactly what Love is, it's power, its creativity or healing aspects. How great it would be to dedicate your life to the study of Love.

For the purposes of this Lesson, we are sharing what we believe Love is and isn't. As you read the following pages, we hope to awaken greater feelings of Love within your heart. The following is the Love Meditation. Each line has been defined and will hopefully instill wonderful new feelings about yourself, your loved ones, and your life. After you have read and understood each of the lines in this meditation, you may then go to the back of the book each time you do your affirmations and Love Meditation.

Explanations of the Love Meditation

1. **I am a Universal Woman, I am Love, I am the feminine aspect of God.** We know that God is Love, therefore all is Love. As women, we are the Love aspect of God, and the Love aspect of humanity. Everything that Love is – We Are. It lies within us.

2. **I am created from the Loving nature of God, the Love nature of all mankind.** Men and women attract each other according to our concepts, which we have built within our minds since childhood. As we become more aware of our own authority and command over life, and stay true to ourselves, we achieve greater actions and reactions to and from each other, thus bonding our relationships with Love.

3. **Love is the substance of my Spirit, mind and body.** As you say this affirmation, try to feel Love in the feeling nature of your emotions, and your physical body. Imagine yourself as a radiating source of Love. Hold that vision.

4. **Love does not force and cannot be forced**. We know that we cannot force any one to love us, respect us, be grateful to us, understand us, or return our love to us. We cannot force our partner to desire us. When force appears, Love disappears. We can demand all of these things, but we would only be creating the pretense of such, which is not inspired by real Love, or genuine tenderness. Likewise, we cannot be forced, and our own decisions must come from wisdom and Love.

5. **Love does not demand, push, order, possess, pressure or manipulate.** We must respect the freedom of all individual's choices. Our own choices must be made through wisdom, Love, and freedom. We may make a request of another person, and they have the right to respond in their own way. Only FEAR pushes, forces, possesses, demands, pressures or manipulates. Only FEAR responds with obedience, or submission.

6. **Love does not hurt nor harm, and cannot be hurt nor harmed.** Love itself can only bring good. When a relationship becomes difficult and feelings are hurt or injured, it is pride or ego, which has been hurt. The truth is Love is impervious to obstacles and continues in spite of appearances to the contrary. You can never hurt another person by loving them.

7. **Love does not reject and cannot be rejected.** Love never dies. Love once recognized, exists forever. It is a vibration that travels the Universe. Even

in the case where a dear one is deceased, or parties have separated for any reason, the Love part of that relationship lives on forever.

8. **Love knows a better way.** The ways of Love are amazing, simple, and often surprising. This is a truth principle that has the potential to change any situation in your life. Surrender any situation to Love, trusting that inner divine guidance which will reveal to you the best answer for your highest good and the good of others. There is no better way than the way of Love.

9. **Love works through free attraction.** This principle draws together friends, families, and mates. It unites collectives, organizations, churches, and the nations of the world. People have tried other methods, but nothing is as lasting as the principle of unity…the free attraction through Love. All else will eventually fail.

10. **Love works through inspiration.** The only way a parent, teacher, or leader can be effective is through inspiration. Any coercion of any kind, is an expression of fear, which leads to resistance and resentment. If you are not achieving the desired results from your children, partner, students, co-workers, etc., remember that power of prayer. Release any dilemma to the power of Universal Love and the perfect answer will come.

11. **The Intelligence of Universal Love is beyond all intellectual understanding.** Love itself knows how to work out any situation in ways beyond our comprehension. If we resolve to put our trust in Love, we will receive its wisdom. We must claim the courage to act upon the wisdom of Love, to the best of our ability – and then watch miracles happen.

12. **Love always expresses perfectly, with freedom, and without fear.** If it is truly Love that you are feeling, you will be guided correctly. Love has its own wisdom, and respects other persons, and of course you, yourself. Love harms no one. Love knows the deepest desires of all concerned and acts for the highest good for all concerned in any situation.

13. **Love is fearless and is acceptance.** Loving acceptance is a powerful magnet which attracts our good to us, including the love of other people. Loving acceptance is irresistible.

14. **Love does not judge and cannot be judged.** Living intelligently we use discernment in our actions and decisions. Love does not judge people. Love sees the best in others. If you hold the attitude of Love, you will enjoy even the smallest expressions of others. Through the eyes of Love, you will see the beauty in everyone.

15. **<u>Love cannot be taken advantage of, because it is willing to give all.</u>** No person, place or thing, can stand in the way of my abundant good. The supply of good is unlimited and cannot be blocked or depleted by the actions of another person.
16. **<u>Love does not withhold and cannot be denied</u>**. It is not in the nature of Love to withhold or repress itself. Love expresses through giving. Love requests and Love receives fulfillment.
17. **<u>Love does not measure and cannot be measured</u>**. Love does not require or measure reciprocity. When you simply become an expression of love for others, you do not regard their ability to return love to you.
18. **<u>Love sets no standards and sees only perfection.</u>** Setting standards for others leads to disappointment. Concentrate on your own perfection of Love, and you will surpass all standards.
19. **<u>Love does not condemn and cannot be condemned.</u>** Love is a vibration which when sent out to others, can dissolve any condemning thoughts held for us. Consciously sending love is a powerful tool and a proven way of ending hatred and turmoil. It can calm a baby or make an angry crowd peaceful. It can even stop violence.

    <u>Note</u>: A number of scientists who have experimented with quantum physics and meditation, have proven that groups of meditators focused on a particular time and place have created positive change including reduction in crime rates, and transforming resistance into cooperation.
20. **<u>Love does not fear and cannot be feared.</u>** When we are determined to express Love and Love only to any person, or into any situation – FEAR disappears.
21. **<u>Love is security.</u>** We can feel relaxed and safe if we are not trying to "get" or "prove" anything. When Love is our motivation we do our best, and gain greater pleasure in all we do.
22. **<u>Love can only enjoy and be enjoyed.</u>** Love's greatest function on the spiritual, mental, emotional, and physical levels is to give Joy. If you can express pure love, uncontaminated by the things which love is not, the pleasure you and yours loved ones will experience will be glorious.

Because Universal Woman *is* Love, women must express love, and be surrounded by love. The whole purpose of this entire course has been to gain a greater understanding of Love.

"If you <u>know</u> these things, blessed are you, if you <u>do</u> them,"

JOHN 13:17

As you study…use and reuse the affirmations, Love, the feminine aspect of God, will be lived by you in ever expanding ways. You will be blessed with happiness, and your experience of inner beauty will grow. As the years go by, you will feel younger, wiser and more self-aware.

Notes

LESSON ELEVEN

The Universal Woman at Work
Love or Fear?

"I will go before thee, and make the crooked places straight."

- Isaiah 45:2

WHETHER YOU HAVE chosen a high powered career with a fabulous income, a part time job to supplement the family income, or a volunteer position with no income, it is important that you stay true to your authentic self.

The same Power that created the CEO – created the Janitor. When you partner with God in all you do, you are automatically empowered for success. Your choice is always Love or Fear. Stop looking at what you think you are not and start praising what you are.

Only your ego can create the idea that you are separate from your Creator in any way. Your subconscious judgements and beliefs about yourself are the determining factor of your success on the job, whether it's in outer space, in the boardroom, or as a stay-at-home mom.

When counseling with Rev. Ann, she often said that Love has an answer to every one of my questions. I needed to go within. Most often I was speaking to her about my marriage. I wish I had used her advice in my business. Sometimes it seemed impossible to see the answers to my problems when they looked like mountains. I needed to identify whether my actions and choices based on Love or Fear. Truthfully, too many were about fear. Okay - No more looking back.

Forgiving yourself is as important as forgiving others. When you are a person who takes responsibility for your actions and outcomes in life, it is easier to stop blaming others for less than stellar results, than it is to stop blaming yourself. *How could I have made that choice? What was I thinking? I've done this before; why the self-sabotage?*

Learn – Let Go – Let's Move On……You'll do better.

Find a prayer partner to lean on while berating yourself for your mistakes. Vent privately, with someone who can respond with supportive, insightful feedback. The CEO needs this – the mother needs this. It is okay to be human AND the more you practice the principles of Love the less you will actually need to vent. Not that you will be less human, but in your humanness you will find gentle reminders to see things differently.

> *"The salve that soothes a broken heart is often the company of a good friend."*
>
> *– DK*

It is essential for women to have Spiritual friendships with other women. Friends that pray together and hold you in prayer during the times when you need it the most, and are bonded with you in Spirit. These deep often life-long friendships help create spiritual maturity. These are reciprocal relationships without record keeping. Every woman needs them.

In the book "The Pathway of Roses", Christian D. Larson writes:

"Do not work for yourself; work for the great idea that stands at the apex of your greatest purpose. The greater idea for which you work, the greater will be your work.

When you begin to live and work for a great purpose, you get into the current of great forces, great minds, and great souls. You gain from every source; all the powerful lives in the world will work with you; you will become a living part of the movement in the world that determines the greater destiny of [humankind]; you become one of the chief elements upon which will depend the future generations yet to be…"

Marsha Sinetar, Educator, Author, Entrepreneur, Consultant, began her professional life as a primary teacher, moved through the ranks of public education as an English teacher, then a K-5 Principal, and soon after a consultant for both local and State projects, designing curriculum for individualized instruction, and mentally gifted minors.

In 1980 she left the public sector to start Sinetar & Associates, Inc., customizing leadership programs for senior management of multinational, Fortune 500 corporations. Concurrently with her private sector work she began writing, and is the author of more than 20 books. In 2000, Sinetar redesigned her life again toward a simpler, more contemplative schedule and began a small R & D arm and Archive related to her lifelong love with what she calls "The True Learning"~ actualizing the spiritual wholeness we are created to be.

In 1987 Marsha wrote a groundbreaking book titled "<u>Do What You Love the Money Will Follow</u>". This book had the audacity to suggest that it was okay to leave the family business or disregard the degree you'd achieved as a safe and secure choice. She suggests that you do what you love for a living – not just as a nice hobby or when the kids have grown and you've retired. This book suggested infusing Love into the work experience. This book which has assisted millions in discovering their right livelihood.

"<u>Elegant Choices ~ Healing Choices</u>" guides readers to grace and wholeness through conscious choices based on love. Both of these books are available in nearly every library and metaphysical bookstore in America. Their Truth is timeless.

Many a commencement speech over the past thirty years has quoted books such as these to empower generations of young women and men to embrace the concept of individual choice based on love and fulfillment in the work place. This has evolved from self-serving love to purpose driven work expressions and today we hear more directives pointed to solving the world's problems. Instead of asking a child *"what do you want to be when you grow up?"* we are to ask *"what problem do you want to solve for the world when you grow up?"*

This idea of reframing our paradigm of the future presents potential growth for all humankind. Children with this perspective will make choices based on love, not fear and the outcomes will ripple out in the oceans of humanity expressing more of the feminine nature. The positively natural consequence will be the reduction of greed, restoration of our planet, and cruelty and war will become an abomination instead of "just a part of life."

This is the work ethic of the Universal Woman.

An excellent example is Mary Therese Winifred Robinson, who was inaugurated as the seventh President of Ireland on December 3, 1990. She became a remarkably popular president, earning the praise of her political opponent Brian Lenihan himself who, before his death five years later, said that she was a better president than he ever could have been. She took an office that had a reputation as being little more than a retirement position for prominent politicians and breathed new life into the role. Robinson brought to the presidency legal knowledge, deep intellect, and political experience. She also brought compassion and willingness for harmony and change.

Mary served her term then attained a post with the United Nations as High Commissioner for Human Rights. She traveled the world championing the rights of women, children, LGBT communities, and immigrants

I first learned of this woman through an NPR interview broadcast regarding an uprising (terrible term for war) in Indonesia. Mary was clearly focused on a tragic scene where very young girls had been sexually molested by soldiers. She was so upset by what she had witnessed that she could barely stay on point during the interview.

Here is a woman who has lived a successful, purposeful life, driven by compassion for all women, without losing her innate feminine feeling nature. This is the potential we possess as we balance both our masculine and feminine natures.

Fifty years ago when Rev. Ann Meyer's original work was published we dreamed of peace on earth by electing women into power. It was never going to happen that way. Women have moved into more power and are working harder than ever. Juggling work, family, partners, the fulfillment of dreams and aspirations has been exhausting. Entire industries have been created to support working women. We cannot, and need not, "do it all".

During the 1960's only 7% of working mothers were the sole income or primary breadwinner as compared to over 40% in today's world. Today, 60% of all women participate in the workforce. There are 31.1 million women in the US workforce and women still average 25% less money than men. How much of this discrepancy is connected our own issues of self-worth?

Women must have faith in themselves, faith in their futures, and faith in their FAITH.

The days of "women firsts" are declining as the pioneering spirit of women has reached into nearly every sector of the work experience worldwide. Some of these firsts, of which we have just recently become aware of are female pioneers who were hidden, and received no open acknowledgement. If you are in a singular or minority position in the workplace, make it your rule to welcome more women into your field.

Supreme Court Justice Ruth Bader Ginsburg who for several years was the court's only female voice, encourages women to work for what you believe in. "… to repair tears in [our] communities, nation, and world, and in the lives of the poor, the forgotten, the people held back because they are members of disadvantaged or distrusted minorities." This woman maintained her groundbreaking position through a bout with cancer, and the loss of the love of her life, Marty Ginsberg.

Working Mother magazine publishes an annual list of their choices for the year's top fifty most powerful mothers. They are not listed based merely on financial success but are a diverse group from a wide variety of personal and professional backgrounds. They are chosen for their successful careers, while paying it forward to motivate their fellow workers, as they work to make the world a better place.

In 2017, the fifty women featured are the mothers of 135 children. The list includes: CEO of Save the Children; CEOs & COOs of nine financial institutions and investment funds; COOs of SpaceX, Facebook, and youtube.com; a TV host, writers, a director, TV producers; actresses and film producers; fashion designers, music industry moguls; community organizers; a National Security Advisor; MDs, scientists, engineers; professors, Senators, an Ambassador; novelists; philanthropists, human rights advocates and an attorney.

Each of the women above are mothers, in relationships, and are highly successful. It is our dream that this book encourages you to release false limitations from your belief systems, so that your soul's journey includes achievements that make a difference in the world. Women constantly create new roles in the workplace. Can you image how these women have balanced the Feminine and Masculine principles within? From all appearances they have MASTERED them. This list is of only fifty women. There are untold numbers achieving the same, in every city, state and country on the planet.

Again, the women mentioned or listed, are from very diverse backgrounds, religions and faiths. Their truths are Universal.

Best of all, we all have access to Divine Mind which can guide us with the same brilliance, the same tenacity, and the same outcomes. We encourage you to explore your dreams with the perspective of the power of Love.

The God we teach is for all people, and is a God of Love, oppressing, repressing, limiting <u>no one</u>. It is much easier to be fearless when you work with the Loving power of the Universe.

> *"You never change things by fighting the existing reality. To change something, build a new model that makes the existing model obsolete."*
>
> – R. Buckminster Fuller - American architect, systems theorist, author, designer, and inventor

Affirmations - Chapter Eleven

Wherever I choose to express my talents and abilities, I do it with Love.

My talents and abilities grow as I continue to deepen my spiritual nature.

I successfully employ my masculine and feminine natures, as necessary.

I know that in the Power and Presence of Love, I am guided, protected, nurtured and inspired.

In the realization of my Oneness with God, I can achieve anything.

My achievements are purposeful and benefit others.

As I serve and support others, I am served and supported.

Notes

LESSON TWELVE

The Universal Woman in the World Spiritual Feminism

FROM ANCIENT TO modern times, women have gathered in talking circles for problem solving, the process of governance, and camaraderie. Everyone has the opportunity to talk, everyone listens. It is thoughtful and powerful. Everyone is served and serving. It is also how we get things done. It is imperative that women continue to have these groups that their lives remain deeply rooted in their spiritual principles. In this way we can move forward on the solid ground of spiritual connectedness.

Kirsten Gillibrand from Time Magazine reported: Tamika Mallory, Bob Bland, Carmen Perez and Linda Sarsour—(this multi ethnic, multi-cultural team) had the courage to take on something big, important and urgent, and never gave up. Because of their hard work, millions of people got off the sidelines, raised their voices and marched. The images of Jan. 21, 2017, show a diverse, dynamic America—striving for equality for all. The moment and movement mattered so profoundly because it was intersectional and deeply personal. *"The Women's March was the most inspiring and transformational moment I've ever witnessed…" writes Gillibrand.*

Having attended one of the worldwide simultaneous marches (San Diego, CA), I was impressed by the peacefulness and joyfulness of it all. Women have and always will come together for high purpose. Senior Editor, Claudia Quinn reports that she attended the same event in Seattle, WA and had the same exact experience. Her niece, who marched in Washington DC, also reported the same results.

Take any women's issue, guide it with spiritual principles, and whether you put out a sign on the street or on the internet, women will show up. It's what we do. The important thing to remember is that what we cannot do ourselves, we can do with God. With regard to supports groups, Louise Hay, author, publisher, spiritual leader, wrote: *"We can make quantum leaps in consciousness together".*

It appears that whenever we try something new, there is opposition. This is when we think we must "fight the good fight". (We call it Polarity) Let's take the "fight" out of it and prepare for opposition with the innate power of spiritual wisdom. As Eleanor Roosevelt wrote, *"Anger is only one letter short of Danger."* Let us transform the "fight" into **Leadership**. We cannot look at opposition as the "enemy" for they may have made choices based on fear. We must find common ground. We must look hard at the opposition and determine whether it is a reflection of fear within. We must be certain of our own choices. The only armament we need is Truth.

The more we practice discernment with Truth, the wider the paths to peace. We must find Love's direction. This does not mean that there will not be hard work. Sometimes there will be mountains to climb and sometimes there will be smooth rivers that flow. Go with God and expect the best. A greater flow of events is more apt to happen through Spirit.

Whatever your faith is, whatever your goal is, whenever you need support, gather a group of women together in a talking circle. Start and end in prayer. Let each woman be heard. Communicate with heartfelt respect and compassion. You will invite wisdom, nurturance and inspiration. The result will be empowerment.

In an award winning video about Mother Teresa, a scene was recorded where she and her rescue team of four are pleading with the military to allow them to enter a war zone and access an abandoned facility where handicapped children and infants have been left to die. The military leaders smiled and were literally fighting back their laughter at her request. They denied her appeal stating that it is far too dangerous for her to enter this battle zone. She is steady in her response and affirms that she will pray to the Virgin Mary that they be allowed to remove these children from their disastrous fate. Again, she is told that this will not be possible and that it is much too dangerous. Her response is that they will return for the children on Thursday morning. It was to be a Feast Day for the Catholic Church.

In the next scene, it is Thursday, an eerily quiet morning, and you see her team enter the building and rescue the children. There is no gunfire. They drive a van full of babies and small children away, quickly and peacefully.

This is a woman who closes her prayers with "Make me your instrument, nothing more…"

Nothing more? She set up sanctuaries in over 60 countries, lifted 42,000 dying people up off the streets of Calcutta, India, and won a Nobel Peace Prize.

This is the way of the Universal Woman. This is the ultimate act of Spiritual Feminism. We can move out of our own grievances and find a way to help others. We can think globally and help sister communities on the other side of the planet or in our own communities.

You are not expected to be another Mother Teresa. There was only one.

You are to become all that YOU are uniquely meant to be.

It is undeniable, YOU are the answer to what happens in the 21st Century.

"Walk in the light, the inner light. Not in my light, but in the light which shines behind the searching, a light so brilliant you would not now dare to look, but it is you. Look for the ease behind your struggling. For you are the thing you seek. You are the joy you wish. Be at peace."

I Have a Dream......

That all women recognize that regardless of age, race, religion, gender identity, or orientation are fully aware of our connectedness through our Creator.

That women delve deeply into their spiritual gifts and share them with others.

I dream that all women have the courage and support to become all that they are meant to be.

I dream that all women gladly raise their sons and daughters to these same standards.

I dream that in the 21 Century the pathways to peace are created by women….

Universal Women.

Now Write Your Dream....

Notes

The Universal Gift

The Masculine & Feminine Natures of Being

Masculine **CAUSE**	*Feminine* **CREATIVE MEDIUM**	*Conclusion* **EFFECT**
THE WORD	UNIVERSAL LAW	MANIFESTATION
THE INTELLECT	THE FEELING	THE EXPRESSION
THE MAN	THE WOMAN	THE CHILD
THE IDEA	THE POWER	THE RESULT
THE CHOICE	THE BELIEF	THE EXPERIENCE

READING THIS CHART from left to right, it reveals is the process of our thoughts and actions. The feminine nature is the creative medium for all the activity of life.

As a whole person, you are all of the Masculine column and the Feminine column. Nothing happens in life without both of these aspects.

All aspects of human nature are to be empowered within you to create the life you desire. This is the Universal Gift to all of humankind.

This is how God designed all of us – Equally.

Affirmations - Lesson One

I am Life – God expressing as a Woman.

I am a complete Male-Female Being, expressing as a Woman.

I am the feminine aspect of God. I am Universal Woman.

I am complete and whole Woman.

I am pure Woman, perfect Woman, and true Woman.

I am free, natural Woman.

I am a unique, individual expression of all Woman.

I am the essence of femininity

Affirmations – Lesson Two

I am all that Universal Woman is.

I am beauty.

I am Love.

I am tenderness and gentleness.

I am warmth.

I am grace.

I am perfect woman form.

I am acceptance.

I am flexibility.

I am receptivity.

I am responsiveness.

I am alluring, magnetic, irresistible Woman.

I am as feminine as any woman who has ever lived.

I am loved and loving, desired and desiring, adored and adoring.

I am a free, perfect expression of Woman Love.

Affirmations - Lesson Three

I know everything a Universal Woman knows. I am balanced and whole.

Feminine Intelligence within me is constantly revealing new truths about the feminine aspect of my true nature. I call forth the Masculine aspect of myself as needed.

I know that I am a completely fulfilled woman. All my needs are met and desires are gloriously fulfilled.

All necessary circumstances and experiences are perfectly created for me by the Law of my Being, which manifests a perfect partner for me, now.

These words set into motion Universal Laws that cannot be denied and therefore manifest according to consciousness –

(Instantaneously, if you are willing)

The Spiritual Feminist

Relationship Equality Meditation

This meditation can be used as a healing tool in any relationship.

Simply enter the name of your partner in the blanks

I am a whole, balanced person of great value, and worthy of every effort for relationship.
I have happiness and fulfillment to share.
My Spirit is a treasure.
My mind is a treasure.
My body is a treasure.
I am precious beyond measure.
I am a treasure for _____ and _____ is a treasure for me.
My partner is of great value to me, and worthy of every effort for relationship.
_____ contributes to my happiness and fulfillment.
_____ Spirit is a treasure for my Spirit.
_____ mind is a treasure for my mind.
_____ body is a treasure for my body.
_____ is precious beyond measure.
_____ is a treasure for me and I am a treasure for _____.

This meditation can neutralize our judgements, and adjust our attitudes about our partner, or a specific person, with whom we may be in relationship. Practice this meditation and watch the dynamic of conflict/resolution change dramatically.

The following is Rev. Ann Meyer's original Man-Woman Relationship Meditation………

The Man-Woman Meditation

This meditation can be used as a healing tool in any relationship. Simply substitute the name of your partner, for the word Man.

I am a treasure for Man.
I am of great value to Man, and worthy of every effort for relationship
I have happiness and fulfillment to give to Man.
My Spirit is a treasure for Man's Spirit.
My mind is a treasure for Man's mind.
My body is a treasure for Man's body.
I am a "Pearl of Great Price"* for Man.
I am precious beyond measure.
I am a treasure for Man and Man is a treasure for me.

Man is a treasure for me.
Man is of great value to me, and worthy of every effort for relationship
Man has happiness and fulfillment to give to me.
Man's Spirit is a treasure for my Spirit.
Man's mind is a treasure for my mind.
Man's body is a treasure for my body.
Man is a "Pearl of Great Price"* for me.
Man is precious beyond measure.
Man is a treasure for me and I am a treasure for Man.

*Matthew 13: 45-46 (A reference to Heaven) *"Who, when he had found one pearl of great price, went and sold all that he had, and bought it."*

Affirmations - Lesson Four

I have all that woman has.

I have an infinite amount of Universal Love.

> *"I have confidence in myself because I have confidence in God. I am sure of myself because I am sure of God."*
>
> JAMES WILLIS, RScP

Affirmations – Lesson Five
The Universal Woman

I am a sensual woman. With love, I praise my womanly body – its sexual organs, its reproductive and hormonal systems.

I give thanks to God for the ability to see the beauty that surrounds me, the beauty in others and the beauty in myself.

Affirmations – Lesson Six
Please add these affirmations to your list and enjoy them daily.

I have all that Universal Woman has.

I have an infinite amount of Woman Love to express.

I praise and love my womb, the secret and hallowed place of creation, the most precious place in every woman's body. It is the treasure of the human race.

I bless the beautiful channel to my womb. It is warm and tender and flowing with love.

I praise the glorious flower of my clitoris, whose only function is to give pleasure to me and my partner.

I love and praise my breasts, belly, my back and buttocks - every part of my ecstatic feminine body.

My physical being expresses, receives and communicates Spiritual Love.

Accepting the Perfect Partner

My Perfect Partner:
_____ is Life, God, expressing as a whole, complete person.
_____ is a Complete Masculine-Feminine Being expressing as a _____.
_____ is created by God, and is honest, perfect and true.
_____ is a unique, natural, individual expression of all_____.

My Perfect Partner:
_____ is all that _____ is created to be.
_____ is beauty, love, warmth, vigor, strength, power, perfect form, assertive, giving, direct, giving, direct, fearless, daring, resilient, joy and wisdom.
_____ is a leader.
_____ is gorgeous, all confident, magnetic and undeniable.

My Perfect Partner
_____ has Universal, ever-present, free, pure, all-intense desire for me.
_____ has a powerful drive to pursue me.
_____ completely accepts me and us as perfect partners.
_____ and we fulfill each other's desires.

My Perfect Partner
_____ knows that we are perfect for each other, spiritually, mentally, and physically. physically.
_____ knows all there is to know about sex and is completely confident in expressing it expressing it with me.
_____ is completely in love with me.
_____ is free from any judgment or rejection of me.
_____ has no barriers between us
_____ accepts me as a perfect mate.
_____ takes a rightful side by side relationship with me.
_____ is self-loving, life-loving and together we express all that we are and all we are meant we are meant to be.

My Perfect Marriage

I THANK GOD, for my perfect marriage. I thank God that the masculine and feminine in me are balanced in a perfect state of understanding, acceptance, love, joy, fascination, excitement, ecstasy and orgasm. This is the truth of my natures as I am a complete, integrated being, a Person of God.

All I desire in a partner, is within me. Nothing can take this away from me. The Unity of my own male/female natures within, creates for my outer life a beautiful expression of unity and love.

I am in Love

I am in love with the perfect partner, and my partner is wholly and completely in love with me. I am complete fulfillment, heaven for my partner, as my partner is for me. I am infinitely valuable to my partner, as my partner is to me. We greatly desire each other. My partner loves to pursue me and I love to be pursued by my partner.

There is absolutely no separation, lack, or rejection between my partner and me. There is only acceptance and joy. There is no fear between my partner and me. We are one in God.

I am free and fulfilled, in all ways.

I am a perfect woman in a perfect love affair, with my perfect partner. We share perfect understanding, communication, expression and fulfillment in Universal Love.

Thank you, God!

Affirmations for Acceptance
Lesson Eight

I embrace acceptance of my own body.

I humbly, and lovingly accept myself and the Goodness of God in my life.

I create new levels of Joy in my life.

I have the sparkle of youth.

I am a free, natural woman and am an instrument of God's Love.

The Love Affirmations
Lesson Ten

1. I am a Universal Woman, I am Love, I am the feminine aspect of God.
2. I am created from the Loving nature of God, the Love nature of all mankind.
3. Love is the substance of my Spirit, mind and body.
4. Love does not force and cannot be forced.
5. Love does not demand, push, order, possess, pressure or manipulate.
6. Love does not hurt nor harm, and cannot be hurt nor harmed.
7. Love does not reject and cannot be rejected.
8. Love knows a better way.
9. Love works through free attraction.
10. Love works through inspiration.
11. The Intelligence of Universal Love is beyond all intellectual understanding.
12. Love always expresses perfectly, with freedom, and without fear.
13. Love is fearless and is acceptance.
14. Love does not judge and cannot be judged.
15. Love cannot be taken advantage of because it is willing to give all.
16. Love does not withhold and cannot be denied.
17. Love does not measure and cannot be measured.
18. Love sets no standards but sees only perfection.
19. Love does not condemn and cannot be condemned.
20. Love does not fear and cannot be feared.
21. Love is my security.
22. Love can only enjoy and be enjoyed.

Affirmations - Chapter Eleven

Wherever I choose to express my talents and abilities, I do it with Love.

My talents and abilities grow as I continue to deepen my spiritual nature.

I successfully employ my masculine and feminine natures, as necessary.

I know that in the Power and Presence of Love, I am guided, protected, nurtured and inspired.

In the realization of my Oneness with God, I can achieve anything.

My achievements are purposeful and benefit others.

As I serve and support others, I am served and supported.

Teaching of the Inner Christ

Our Philosophy
The Teaching of the Inner Christ (T.I.C.) is a non-profit, non-denominational spiritual teaching which helps you to contact and experience your True Self, your God Center, your "Christ Self" within, which is your own individual inner spiritual identity.

Other Course Books available on our website:
Being a Christ - by Rev. Ann & Rev. Peter Meyer
Self Mastery in the Christ Consciousness – by Rev. Ann Meyer
Being A Christ - Audio Book – by Rev. Ann Meyer
Holy Bible - The Aramaic Interpretation - by George Lamsa
Hidden Mystery of the Bible – by Jack Addington
See website for full list of available books

T.I.C. Locations
<u>El Cajon, CA – (Headquarters)</u>
1114 North Second Street
El Cajon, CA 92021 619.447.7007 elcajon@innerchrist.org
<u>Long Beach, CA</u>
1775 Bellflower Blvd
Long Beach, CA 90815 562.498.9211 longbeach@innerchrist.org
<u>Las Vegas, NV</u>
lasvegas@innerchrist.org
<u>Outreach Online Ministry</u>
The TIC Outreach Ministry that provides online classes. 619.200.3639 online@innerchrist.org
Website - www.teachingoftheinnerchrist.org

Biography of Rev. Ann Meyer, DD

Born Ann Porter Remington, in 1916, Ann spent her childhood Minnesota. She owned her first Bible at the age of ten and studied it diligently for years, scribbling her own notes and revelations in the margins. She was talented musically as well as intellectually advanced. At the age of 16, Ann entered Coker College in Hartsville, South Carolina, where she studied piano, voice and her primary love - composition. She became an accomplished musician and composer. After graduation she married William Rosser. They moved to New York City where she established herself as an opera singer. She also discovered a marvelous teacher, orator and author, Emmet Fox, and traveled by train from the suburbs weekly to attend his lectures on the Principles of New Thought at Carnegie Hall.

Ann and her husband had four children and eventually moved the family to San Diego, where she starred in operettas presented by Starlight Opera. She also performed as a soloist in several churches and synagogues, one of which was the San Diego Church of Religious Science. Spiritually aware and interested in metaphysics, she later completed the course work to become a licensed Religious Science Practitioner in 1960. William and Ann ultimately parted ways as she pursued a new and dedicated path to a deeper understanding of God within her and what was to become her life's ministry.

About this time, she began to experience a powerful spiritual phenomena (which is fully described in her last book "Who Is With Me?"). On October 19, 1962, she was visited by the Yogi Master Babaji, in physical form. He sat beside her during a symphony concert, appearing as a normal man, but through many paranormal events that evening, he awakened her to a revolutionary new teaching that everyone is a unique individual Christ, after the example of Jesus. Babaji had opened a "Power Door" from the vibration of Spirit down to the vibration of earth. Ann realized at that moment that this was the purpose for which she was born -- to bring through this brand new teaching and to give it to others so that all may grow in awareness of their own Christhood.

In 1963, Ann married Peter Meyer and together they formed "Society for the Teaching of the Inner Christ". Both had been experiencing inner teaching and guidance from Babaji, separately. Channeling from Babaji and Jesus and other masters including their own Inner Christ Selves, they developed a curriculum and began teaching. At present, thousands of students all over the world have healed themselves and enriched their lives through taking the T.I.C. courses.

Rev. Ann was ordained in 1966 and earned the Degree of Doctor of Divinity in 1969. Her life story can be found in her book "Who Is With Me?" which is available at all T.I.C. Centers as well as in the website store. At the age of 91, Ann transitioned to the next phase of her glorious mission on September 4, 2007.

Bibliography & Recommended Reading

Behrand, Genevieve, 2015 - The Collection – A Timeless Wisdom Book

Byrnes, Rhonda, 2010 - The Power

Canfield, Jack & Watkins, D.D. 2007, Key to Living the Law of Attraction

Carmon, Irin & Knizhnik, Shan, 2017 - Notorious RBG: The Life and Times of Ruth Bader Ginsburg

Ferrini, Paul:
    1994 - Love Without Conditions, 1996 – The Silence of The Heart
    1998 - Grace Unfolding., 2000 – Reflections of the Christ Mind

Ferrucci, Piero, 2009 - Beauty and the Soul

Fromm, Erich, 2006 - The Art of Loving

Hay, Louise, 1984 - You Can Heal Your Life

Hanh, Thich Nhat, 1991 - Old Path White Clouds by Thich Nhat Hanh

Johnson, Deborah, 2006 - The Sacred Yes

King Jr., Martin Luther, 2010 Reissue - Why We Can't Wait

Larson, Christian, 1918 - The Pathway of Roses – The Timeless Wisdom Book

Maitland, Sara, 1996 - A Big Enough God

Mother Teresa, 1989 - No Greater Love

Northrup MD, Christiane, 2015 - Goddesses Never Age

Ritz, David Owen, 1998 - Keys to The Kingdom

The Shanti Christo Foundation, 2005 through 2012:
    The Way of Mastery Part One – The Way of the Heart
    The Way of Mastery Part Two – The Way of Transformation
    The Way of Mastery Part Three – The Way of Knowing

Smith, Huston, 1995 – Illustrated World Religions: A Guide to Wisdom Traditions

Steinem, Gloria, 2015 – My Life on The Road

Walsh MD, Roger, 2010 - Essential Spirituality – Exercises from World's Religions

Williamson, Marianne, 2010 - A Course in Weight Loss

Acknowledgements

THERE ARE NO words to describe the depth of my gratitude for the honor of co-writing this book. I, of myself did nothing but to convey the inspirations given to me in its own process. I know that Rev. Ann, the Masters and Angels were with me page by page.

The Women of the International Board of Trustees, for the Teaching of the Inner Christ were wonderfully supportive. Rev. Kayla Rose, Rev. Mary Ann Kelly, Rev. Elizabeth Brabant, Rev. Brigitte Heimers and Rev. Rhonda Hawley. Each of them attended meetings, reviewed unedited manuscripts, and said it was good anyway. In the end, they had the authority to do anything they wanted with it. We proceeded with love, because they trusted the process. Thank you God, for these beautiful women.

Thank you to my wonderful Senior Editor, Claudia Quinn who gently reminded me of that no manuscript needs three hundred exclamation points, which actually spoke to my enthusiasm while in this writing process. I had no idea… Claudia, with great kindness asks thought provoking questions. I'll love you forever, will keep you for always…

More gratitude goes to Kay Prior, whose thoroughness and wisdom always makes me proud to work with her no matter what the project. Everyone should have a Kay…

When looking for another type of editor, with a younger viewpoint and no connection to a metaphysical organization, I found Wendy Marcot. As an educator, she has a great sense of correctness. As a beautiful soul, she asked all the questions needed to open this dialogue to a wider audience. Now, I want to adopt her…

Heartfelt thanks for the support of Rev. Sharon Hudson, who actually new Rev. Ann Meyer and still had her copy of the original Woman Awareness book. She is Love walking…

Sincere gratitude to Rev. Katherine Economou and all my CSL family, especially the Ladies of the Book Study, whom after reading my other books, strongly encouraged the work on this one. You make my heart sing!

About the Cover... I chose the Acanthus Leaf because it represents diversity, it is the mother plant to thirty species in the Mediterranean region. To me, diversity is an infinite gift from our Creator. The cover came together through the talented graphic artist Molly Jimenez. Molly herself is a jewel in the art of creative diversity. Mother love walking...

In my spiritual journey, I have found and loved a Unity family, a CSL family and a T.I.C. family, and because of them my children have thrived. I also was incredibly fortunate to grow up in the strong foundation of my Lutheran family. Love is my religion.

Your Notes: